The American Colonies
Table of Contents

Early French Colonization

With the first voyage of the great Italian explorer Christopher Columbus to the Western Hemisphere in 1492, his sponsoring nation, Spain, became the first European power to stake a serious claim to the New World—its land, its riches, and its people.

Other nations, however, jealous of the success of Spain's colonizing efforts in the Americas, soon followed with voyages of their own to the lands west of the Atlantic Ocean. England challenged first, with the voyages of John Cabot. His first trip to America occurred in 1497. He landed at Newfoundland in modern-day Canada. He sailed again in 1498, but the English proved slow in following up on Cabot's discoveries.

The French followed next, sending another Italian explorer, Giovanni da Verrazano to the New World in 1524, where he landed along the coast of South Carolina and sailed north along the coast to Newfoundland. Verrazano was intent on discovering an all-water route through the Western Hemisphere to the Orient, but failed. (No such route exists.) Jacques Cartier, also sailing under French sponsorship, followed a decade later. On his second voyage, he tried to establish a colony in Canada, but this effort was unsuccessful.

Each of these explorers—Cabot, Verrazano, Cartier—failed to discover either of their two significant goals as explorers. They did not discover the "Northwest Passage" through the Western Hemisphere to the Far East, nor did they find gold in any significant amounts. For the time being, the treasures of the New World were in the hands of the Spanish. Extensive mines in Mexico and modern-day Peru were extracting literally tons of both gold and silver for the Spanish crown. Great treasure ships filled with both precious metals regularly sailed from New World Spanish colonies to Spain throughout most of the 1500s.

Having failed at colonizing in Canada and in finding gold in North America, the French turned to another approach to gaining riches in the New World. Spanish treasure ships, bound for Spain,

typically sailed through the Straits of Florida, south of the peninsula itself, then made their way through a narrow channel between the Florida mainland and the Bahama Islands. This route placed such ships on the Gulf Stream, a constant circuit of flowing water.

The French determined to gain New World gold by stealing it from the Spanish. To that end, they established a colony along the North American coast. The colony's sponsor was Gaspard de Cologny, a highly influential and wealthy French Protestant who was also an admiral in the French Navy. He employed a career naval officer, Jean Ribaut, to lead the colonizing effort.

Early in the spring of 1562, Ribaut sailed to America with three ships and approximately 150 colonists, mostly Huguenots (French Protestants). On May 1, the expedition reached the mouth of the St. John's River in Florida, and Ribaut claimed it for the French crown. (The Spanish would later establish a settlement there called St. Augustine.)

The party continued northward, looking for a more suitable spot for their colony. Ribaut selected a site on the southern portion of Port Royal Island, in modern-day South Carolina. The colonists began building a garrison, and were soon tantalized by Native Americans in the region who spoke of great cities of gold located just 20 days journey to the west. Perhaps great riches lay ahead for the first French colony in North America.

French Failure at Charlesfort

The French colonists in the New World named their settlement Charlesfort. Now they were intent on Indian stories about great, wealthy cities of gold to the west. But more important questions rose as the colony began to take shape.

For many of the colonists, the challenges they faced in the New World were no greater than those they faced back home in France. They were French Protestants, Huguenots, and they were regularly persecuted in France because of their beliefs. (Most of the people and the leaders in France were Catholics.) These Huguenots had signed on to come to America in search of a world where they could practice their religion without being imprisoned or killed.

At first, the colonists' efforts proceeded with success. They met with local Indians and made peaceful relations with them, trading regularly. Ribaut described the Native Americans in the region as "very gentle, courteous, and of good nature."

But the colony soon experienced problems. They had not brought adequate supplies, and soon began to run low on food and ammunition. The colonists had not even brought enough farming tools. Many had not considered they would become farmers, especially those who were, by trade, sailors.

With no choice, Ribaut determined to sail to France where he would get fresh provisions and return to Charlesfort. Many decided to return with him. Only about 30 agreed to stay in the New World wilderness. However, when he arrived home on July 20, 1562, he discovered France embroiled in a religious war. Ribaut was unable to return immediately. This only helped to spell doom for the French colony at Charlesfort.

For a while, the colonists were able to convince the local Indians to provide them with food. But, in time, they stopped feeding the Frenchmen. The situation became desperate for the colonists. Some of the men argued, and the disputes led some to kill their leader. Starving, many of them sick and weak, the Huguenot colonists made a desperate decision. They built a small boat, intent on sailing back to France across the great open expanse of the Atlantic. Using their shirts and other clothing for sails, the colonists abandoned Charlesfort and began their adventure home. (One colonist, a youth of 16, decided to remain at Charlesfort. He was taken in by Indians and later rescued by the Spanish.) Having already experienced real hunger, the voyage only made circumstances worse. Emaciated and malnourished, the men ate their leather shoes. When one of the men died, the others practiced cannibalism, consuming their dead comrade's flesh. Finally, drifting aimless on open sea, the last of the party on the verge of death, they were spotted by an English ship and taken to London.

The French colonists were seen as great adventurers, and they were given an audience with Queen Elizabeth I. The men raved about the New World, speaking of its great wealth and beauty. They described a world abundant with gold, silver, and spices. The English were eager to hear such tales, which included a story of mining precious jewels at night because they glistened so brightly by day that they blinded the men.

As chance would have it, Ribaut also appeared in England, driven out of France by the religious war. He, too, met Elizabeth I and told of his experiences in the New World. In 1563, he published an account titled, Whole and True Discovery of Terra Florida. His book was widely read in England and convinced English adventurers to attempt their own colonies in the New World.

Review and Write

1. What problems plagued the French colonists at Charlesfort?

2. Describe the role Jean Ribaut played in the early French colony of Charlesfort. Include in your answers his relations with Native Americans.

3. Why did Ribaut leave the Charlesfort Colony in 1562 and sail to France?

New Spanish Settlements in Florida

While the colonizing efforts of the French Huguenots in the Americas failed, they did manage to inspire an entire generation of English explorers intent on establishing their own presence in the Western Hemisphere.

It was the end of Ribaut's efforts in the New World, however. In 1565, Admiral Cologny sent him back to America on a second voyage, this time with seven ships, to resupply a colony which had been established by another French adventurer, René de Laudonnière in 1564. The colony had been erected at Ribaut's original landing site on the St. John's River in Florida. (Today it is the site of Jacksonville, Florida.)

The colony, called Fort Caroline, was established as a base for menacing Spanish treasure ships that sailed in nearby waters. But the Spanish were determined not to allow the French settlement to remain a threat.

A Spanish naval commander, Pedro Menendez de Aviles (ah-VEE-lace) sailed from Spain in the summer of 1565 bound for the New World. Accompanying him were 1,500 Spanish colonists. They were to establish a colony in Florida to provide protection for Spanish ships sailing in the region. In addition, Menendez intended to destroy the French presence at Fort Caroline.

He established his colony just 50 miles south of the French settlement and named it St. Augustine. Wasting little time, Menendez marched north for three days, amid torrential rains, intending to destroy Fort Caroline. When the Spaniards attacked, the French were unprepared. The fight lasted less than an hour and ended with the massacre of most of the Huguenots. Some escaped, sailed to France and reported on the massacre they had suffered at the hands of the Spanish.

When the Spanish attacked Fort Caroline, Ribaut was not there. Just as Menendez intended to destroy the French colony, Ribaut organized a party to eliminate the Spanish settlement at St. Augustine. However, en route, a hurricane destroyed his ship, leaving Ribaut and his men stranded on an island. In time, they were found by Menendez and his soldiers, who murdered the marooned Frenchmen. Only two French Catholics were allowed to live.

The destruction of Fort Caroline was a great blow to the French. Many in France were shocked at the massacres, for the French and Spanish were at peace at that time. The losses of both Charlesfort and Fort Caroline brought an end to any serious French colonial efforts in the New World for the remainder of the 1500s.

Having removed the French presence, the Spanish built a series of forts along the eastern seaboard from Florida to South Carolina. They erected Fort San Mateo on the former site of Fort Caroline. The Spanish even sent five priests to the region of the Chesapeake Bay to establish a mission settlement and convert the local Native Americans.

But Spain's sea-going treasure ships were not completely safe, nor were her Atlantic Coast colonies. While the French no longer posed a challenge, the English soon would.

Such English captains—often called "sea dogs" — began raiding Spanish ships and menacing their colonies. One English sea dog, Francis Drake, attacked the Spanish fort, Santa Elena, in 1586. (It had been built just south of the former French colony of Fort Caroline.) Soon the English found themselves ready to attempt permanent colonization in America. As with the French, their early efforts proved difficult.

Review and Write

1. While the French colony at Charlesfort ultimately failed, the French soon established another colony along the Atlantic coast, this time at Fort Caroline. What was the purpose of Fort Caroline?

2. How did the loss of the French colonies at Charlesfort and Fort Caroline impact French colonization in North America?

England Challenges Spain

During the 1500s, the Spanish and French competed fiercely for territory in the New World—from Brazil to the Hudson Bay.

Preoccupied domestically, the English were slow to join the race. Their inability to challenge Spain at sea also contributed to their delay and forced them to route their ships far to the north of New Spain when they finally crossed the Atlantic just before the end of the 16th century.

English fishermen established villages off Newfoundland where they caught cod and other fish by the ton. In time, they were busy trading with the local Indians, offering iron cooking kettles, shiny mirrors, European hammers, and dozens of other manufactured items in exchange for American furs.

By the late 1500s, intrepid Englishmen—courtiers to the Queen, such as Sir Humphrey Gilbert and Sir Walter Raleigh, as well as sea captains such as John Hawkins and Francis Drake—began to challenge Spanish power in the Caribbean.

One of the first to move against the Spanish was John Hawkins. The son of a merchant, he arrived in the Spanish Caribbean in 1562 and sold black slaves he had picked up on an earlier voyage to West Africa to Spanish plantation owners. When Hawkins returned in 1565 to repeat such trade, Spanish authorities attempted to shut him out. But Hawkins slipped in, and once again traded with Spanish traders. During another attempt, Spanish officials dispatched warships to intercept Hawkins, resulting in a pitched sea battle in which he lost three of his five ships. Only his own and another captained by his cousin, Francis Drake, managed to escape.

Over the next twenty years, relations between the Spanish and English deteriorated. The King of Spain, Philip II—brother-in-law to Queen Elizabeth I—complained bitterly to the English monarch as English ships menaced his colonies and attacked his treasure ships.

At the center of the developing rivalry between Elizabeth I and Philip II was the religious movement called the Reformation. Philip ruled his nation as a strong Catholic monarch, while Elizabeth gave support to the Protestant movement. This religious antagonism guaranteed that the two rulers would rarely see eye to eye.

By 1577, Queen Elizabeth let loose Francis Drake on the Spanish. Drake was given six ships and permission to menace the Spanish at will. He terrorized Spain's colonies along the South American coast, then sailed around Cape Horn and then raided Spanish settlements in Chile and Peru. At the same time, he raided Spanish treasure ships along the way.

Knowing that if he returned to the Atlantic, the Spanish would be waiting for him, Drake pushed off across the Pacific, harassing the Spanish in the Philippines. Then he picked up a cargo of spices at the Molucca Islands, and returned home.

While such raids brought great treasure to England, they did not help to establish English colonies in the New World. It would take another group of Englishmen to accomplish this more long-term New World effort.

Review and Write

How did Englishmen such as John Hawkins challenge Spanish authority and power in the New World?

Elizabethan Exploration

While English sea pirates such as Francis Drake and John Hawkins roamed the high seas in search of Spanish treasure—exploits that managed to get both men knighted—other men remained at home with growing intentions of founding permanent colonies in the New World.

One of the early leaders of the English colonization movement was Sir Humphrey Gilbert. He became convinced that the best way to meet the Spanish challenge in the New World was to establish a string of fortified colonies north of the Spanish colonies which would serve as a blockade against the Spanish colonization further north.

In addition, Gilbert wrote a small book, titled Discourse of a Discovery for a New Passage to Catia, which was published in the 1570s. The purpose of the volume was to convince others, including Queen Elizabeth, of the possibilities of the yet undiscovered "Northwest Passage." Gilbert also announced his intentions to convert the Native Americans to Protestantism. All he asked in return for his plans was that he be allowed to keep any treasure he discovered in the New World for himself.

Queen Elizabeth responded positively to Gilbert's suggestions by outfitting several voyages of exploration. Gilbert did not sail initially himself, but rather it was for Martin Frobisher, one of the England's best sea captains, to make the first voyage.

Sir Martin Frobisher set sail in search of the Northwest Passage in 1576. He sailed further north than had earlier explorers, examining the coastline of Baffin Island for a route through to the Orient. He never found one. Intent on discovering riches, Frobisher searched not only for the Northwest Passage, but for gold as well. On Baffin Island, he picked great quantities of metal ore he believed contained gold. He was wrong.

But his voyage inspired English gold seekers everywhere, and prompted Queen Elizabeth to finance a second voyage. (Frobisher had returned with an Inuit male, which he believed proved he was near China.) His second voyage produced little, as well. A third voyage was mounted in 1578. This time, he returned with over a thousand tons of glittering ore which he, once again, believed contained gold. But instead he was disappointed to find that the ore was only iron pyrite, a metal otherwise known today as "fool's gold."

Frobisher's third would be his last. Gilbert's dream of discovering a Northwest Passage, of establishing colonies, of unearthing great riches in the New World remained a dream. Disappointed in Frobisher, Gilbert determined to make a voyage to the New World himself. Queen Elizabeth agreed, and, in 1578, she granted Gilbert charter allowing him six years exclusive right to establish a colony in the Americas.

Gilbert's first attempt to sail to America in 1578 failed when violent storms caused him to turn his seven ships manned by 400 Englishmen back home to England. A lack of money caused him to delay five years before making a second attempt. In 1583, he made his second attempt, having pledged the family fortune to pay for the venture. While he did land at Newfoundland, storms once again struck. Gilbert's ship was lost at sea and along with it the man with the dream of English colonies in the New World.

Review and Write

What problems did Frobisher and Gilbert face in exploring the New World?

Raleigh Sponsors a Colony

Sir Humphrey Gilbert's dream of discovering the Northwest Passage and great wealth in the New World seemed lost when he drowned at sea during a severe storm. But his dreams continued when his half-brother, Sir Walter Raleigh, took up Sir Humphrey's cause.

Gilbert's plan to establish a proprietary colony in the New World did not die. His idea had been to build such a colony in the Americas where he would serve as proprietor, a leader who governed his lands in the name of the English king or queen, and profited greatly from his efforts. Although Gilbert himself failed, other English colonies in North America—including Maryland, the Carolinas, New York, and Pennsylvania—all sprang from dreams similar to those of Gilbert.

More directly, Gilbert's colonial plans were immediately picked up by his half-brother, Sir Walter Raleigh. He was very much like his brother. Both men were loyal supporters of her majesty, Queen Elizabeth. Both had fought to establish Protestantism in Ireland. But when Raleigh ordered the hanging of a dozen Catholic women, some of whom were pregnant, he was denied a land grant in Ireland for his overzealous efforts.

Still wanting land and wealth, Raleigh returned to England and requested the right to take over his half-brother's charter to establish a colony in the New World. Still a favorite of the queen, Elizabeth granted him the privilege of taking up Gilbert's cause.

Raleigh began immediately drumming up support for his colony. He needed to make his vision one that other people would believe in. Such an effort would require all kinds of skills, not to mention the ships, captains, and sailors to make the voyage across the Atlantic.

By 1584, Raleigh had recruited men to sail to America on a reconnaissance mission. The English knew little of the lands along the Atlantic seaboard of North America. Raleigh needed to know where the colony should be located. This purpose of the first voyage was to scout along the coast in search of a good site for a colony.

Two small ships sailed from England in April bound for the New World. They landed at the Caribbean island of Puerto Rico first, then sailed north to the Carolina coast. There the explorers found a land having a "strong and sweet smell." They landed at an island off the coast of modern-day North Carolina occupied by Indians called the Roanoke. The natives impressed the Englishmen, who described them as "most gentle, loving and faithful . . . [living] after a manner of the golden age." When they reported back to Raleigh, he named the land "Virginia," in honor of the Virgin Queen. (Elizabeth had never married.)

The following year, a second expedition made its way to Roanoke Island. The party consisted of seven ships and 100 men. Their plan was to establish a colony on Roanoke. Among the colonists was an artist named John White, who sketched many pictures of the Native Americans he encountered in the New World. Other men on the expedition included writer and poet, Thomas Harriot and a Jewish mineral expert, Joachim Ganz. His job was to search for gold and silver. Still others were carpenters, farmers, winemakers, and druggists.

From the beginning, the men found their work in the New World difficult. Storms battered the island, and they arrived too late to plant crops. Nearly starving, they were picked up a year later by Francis Drake and returned to England. Raleigh's first attempt at a New World colony had failed.

Review and Write

1. Several English colonizers attempted to establish proprietary colonies in the New World. What was a "Proprietary colony" and where did Sir Walter Raleigh attempt to establish one?

2. After the failures of Sir Humphrey Gilbert in the New World, how did his half-brother, Sir Walter Raleigh, attempt to pick up where Gilbert left off?

Roanoke: The Lost Colony

The first colony established in Raleigh's "Virginia," had, within a year of its founding, proven a failure. Many problems contributed to its end. For one, the colony never became self-sufficient. The colonists relied too heavily on food from the local Indians, and the natives soon became concerned about their dwindling food supply.

When the local tribal leader, Wingina, cut off the colonists' food supply, the colonial commander, a military captain named Ralph Lane, attacked the local village in the spring of 1586. During the assault, Lane killed the chief of the Roanokes, causing a permanent rift between the two sides. When Francis Drake sailed into the area a month later, the remaining colonists were ready to abandon the colony for fear of their lives.

After the colonists abandoned their fort and sailed back to England, a supply fleet sent by Raleigh arrived to find the colony abandoned. But before the ships sailed away, a few volunteers were left behind to search for the missing colonists.

Although Raleigh's attempt from 1585 to 1586 to establish an English colony in the New World failed, he was not completely discouraged. He learned from his mistakes, recalculated, and immediately began planning another attempt. He realized it would be hard to convince others to go to the New World after the failure of the first colony. To make the colony more appealing to would-be emigrants, Raleigh allowed not only men to participate, but their wives, children, and servants as well.

In April 1587, Raleigh had lined up enough colonists and backers to support his New World dream. The number included 150 men, plus an unknown number of family members, including two pregnant wives. Among those Raleigh recruited was John White, the artist who had participated in the previous colonization venture. In fact, White and Thomas Hariot produced a book titled *Brief and True Report of the New Found Land of Virginia* (White provided the illustrations) that helped advertise the prospects of a new colony in the Americas.

At last, everything seemed to be in place for the establishment of a new colony, one Raleigh intended to name after himself—"The City of Raleigh." The party set sail, bound for the New World, unaware of the fate that awaited them.

Raleigh had ordered the ship's captain, Simon Fernandez, to land the party north of Roanoke Island (to avoid the Indians now hostile to the English), somewhere in the Chesapeake Bay. But Fernandez dumped the colonists off in the area of the previous colony, so he could sail south and raid Spanish treasure ships.

From the beginning, things went badly. The colonists arrived too late in the spring to plant crops. They spent too much time looking for gold and too little time gathering food and building shelters. The settlers soon begged White to return to England to bring back fresh supplies. White remained in the colony until his married daughter gave birth to his granddaughter, Virginia Dare, the first English baby born in the New World.

White did return to England, but his voyage back to the colony was delayed when war broke out between England and Spain. In fact, he did not return to Roanoke until 1590. What he found gave him great sadness. The entire colony had disappeared, including his daughter, son-in-law, and granddaughter. On a post, he found the word *CROATAN* carved into the wood, (the Croatoans were a local Indian tribe) but what happened to the colonists of the "Lost Colony of Roanoke" has never been determined.

Review and Write

1. How did an early reliance on food provided by local Indians ultimately make for later problems for the Roanoke colonists?

2. Raleigh's first colonizing effort at Roanoke proved to be a failure. What lessons did Raleigh learn from that experience that helped him establish a new colony in the New World?

The Popham Colony

Even before the news of the "Lost Colony of Roanoke" reached Sir Walter Raleigh, he had decided to give up on New World colonization. His experiences told him there was no quick route to riches or colonization in North America. In 1589, he granted the right to colonize his "Virginia" to a group of 19 investors, most of them wealthy London merchants. But no one attempted a new colonizing effort for the rest of the 1500s. As Raleigh himself wrote, "No man makes haste to the market where there is nothing to be bought but blows."

But for all the challenges the New World represented to the English, the lure of American colonies continued to draw interest. The French were having some limited success in Canada, and the English did not wish to be left without a foothold in the Americas. By 1602, English traders made their way back to the New World.

Most of the original ventures were financed privately, without monetary backing from Queen Elizabeth or, after her death in 1603, King James I. They did not return to Roanoke, but, instead, far to the north. Early arrivals explored the region of modern-day Massachusetts and Maine, looking for furs and cedar trees.

Their first efforts were generally unsuccessful. The English, unlike the French further north, often mistreated the Indians they came into contact with, thus making trade difficult. One such trip, in 1605, serves as an example.

In that year, a merchant named George Weymouth came to Maine in 1605 to establish a trading post. But the Abenaki Indians refused to trade with the English, preferring the French instead. Weymouth refused to take "no" for an answer. He lured some Abenakis onboard his ship, only to seize five of them by the hair, taking them as captives. He then left the region and returned with his prisoners to England.

In 1606, another English merchant expedition returned to Maine, along with three of the five Abenaki captives. They were sponsored by a group of wealthy investors called the Plymouth Company, which held the rights to colonize between Maine and the Potomac River in modern-day Virginia. Another group of English investors, the London Company, had received rights to colonize between modern-day New York City and North Carolina.

The leader of the expedition, Martin Pring, chose a site for the party's trading post at the mouth of the Kennebec River, a place the local natives called Sagadahoc. The chief justice of England, Sir John Popham, provided much of the backing for the colony.

The next year, a group of more than 40 men arrived at the new site to colonize the region. George Popham, a relative of Sir John, and Raleigh Gilbert, 24-year old son of Sir Humphrey, provided the leadership. Problems abounded. Popham died before the end of the first winter, and a fire destroyed much of the colony's supplies.

When relations with local Indians deteriorated, due mostly to mistreatment by the English, the colony collapsed. Those who survived the harsh winter of 1607-08 built a small ship of thirty tons and returned to Plymouth, England. Before their departure, nearly half of the colony's inhabitants had died.

Review and Write

Why were the Roanoke and Popham colonies ultimately unsuccessful?

Establishing a Virginia Colony

Even before the founding of the Popham Colony in Maine, another English colonization effort was being organized. Those London merchants who comprised the London Company became convinced they could succeed in the New World despite the odds. Their efforts began in 1606 when the company was formed. At the time, the merchants requested a charter for New World settlement from King James I. Once royal permission was granted, the London, or Virginia, Company began looking to America.

Unlike the Spanish monarchs who, for over a century, had financed and underwritten the cost of New World exploration and colonization, King James and others who followed him on the English throne, did not invest money in colonizing efforts. Therefore, the Virginia Company raised its own capital. As a joint-stock company, the merchants sold shares of stock to investors willing to gamble on a New World venture. The money raised provided funds for the purchase of ships, supplies, and the recruitment of colonists.

Late in December 1606, three small ships left England bound for America: the 120-ton *Susan Constant*, the 40-ton *Godspeed*, and the 20-ton pinnance *Discovery*. (The smaller *Discovery* was intended for use as an exploration boat once the party arrived in the New World.) Aboard the three ships were 144 settlers, all male, including four boys. The party included a wide variety of passengers: common laborers, as well as a surgeon, blacksmith, carpenter, barber, minister, perfumer, tailor, goldsmiths, bricklayers, and soldiers. There were also gentlemen unaccustomed to work, intent on finding gold in the New World.

The expedition included a military leader named John Smith. His involvement in the colony would prove invaluable. The 26-year-old Smith was a seasoned soldier who fought the Turks in Eastern Europe. Captain Christopher Newport, one of the most skilled sea mariners of his day, guided the ships across the Atlantic. After a long and difficult voyage, the ships reached the Virginia coast on

April 26, 1607. During the passage, 39 members of the group died. The remaining party members began a search for a good site for their fort and colony. They were under instructions to establish the colony along a river narrow enough for their cannons to hit an enemy ship in mid-stream, yet wide enough to accommodate ocean-going supply ships.

Captain Newport selected a potato-shaped peninsula covered with woods and grasses 50 miles up a river that would soon be named the James after the English monarch. "James Island" was home to the colonists and sailors. Soon construction began on shelters for the colony that they called Fort James.

Without a doubt, Newport's selection of the James Island site was a poor one. While its 800 acres might provide rich farmland, it was a swampy place, and disease-carrying mosquitoes were a constant problem. Also, the peninsula was situated where the river's fresh water mingled with the seawater of the Atlantic. This caused the peninsula's ground-water to hold nearly all the human waste produced by the colonists. In time, the men at Fort James were drinking and washing in polluted water, which brought on more disease. The chances of surviving their first winter in Virginia looked no more promising than it had for the Popham Colony.

Review and Write

Several occupations of those who sailed to the New World are given on this page. What skills noted might have come in handy at Fort James? What occupations may have been unnecessary?

Troubles for Fort James

Once the men had reached the James Island site, they began immediately to organize their efforts in three directions. One group was chosen to build a fort and housing. Another group was selected to clear land for planting. Meanwhile, a third party began exploring the James River as a possible passage to the Far East.

Soon, however, problems developed. The colonists had consumed more of their food supply during the voyage than had been planned, thus making food scarce. The settlers had intended to plant experimental crops, such as melons, cotton, potatoes, and orange trees, but did not plant much of a grain crop. They also arrived too late to plant an early crop. Disease began to infest the colony. Malaria-carrying mosquitoes infected the men, producing a string of sick and dying colonists. Dysentery and typhoid, diseases bred by contaminated water, added to the settlers' misery. In time, men were dying at the rate of one or two almost every day.

Social class differences also created problems in the Fort James settlement. About one-third to one-half of the colonists were English gentlemen, unaccustomed to taking orders or working with their hands. Most of these men were intent on searching for gold, while those of lesser social rank performed the labor. But the settlement, to survive, needed the labor of all its residents.

Indian relations also deteriorated. The Paspahegh, natives belonging to an Indian confederation of tribes called the Powhatan Confederation, claimed James Island and did not like the English settlers

building a permanent fort on the site. When a scouting party of Englishmen traveled up the James River and gave gifts to a enemy tribe of the Paspaheghs, the Weanocs, the Paspaheghs attacked the settlement.

By August 1607, Fort James was home to only five or six healthy inhabitants. The remainder were dead or ill. By January 1608, only 38 men remained alive out of the 144 who had left England a year earlier.

Fortunately, Captain Newport, who had left the colony to fetch supplies in England, returned the same month, bringing with him 120 new colonists. But just five days after his arrival, a fire "consumed all the buildings of the fort and storehouse of ammunition and provisions." Only three buildings remained to house the colonists during the coldest months of the year.

Eventually, the colonists turned to John Smith for leadership. Smith had fallen out of favor with the colony's leaders early on and had been excluded from much of their plans. But, with the inhabitants of Fort James dying, Smith provided a forceful presence. He put everyone to work, even the gentlemen, telling them, "He that will not worke shall not eate." When Smith caught wind of a plot among the colonists to abandon the colony for England, he ordered the leader tried for treason and shot.

In addition, Smith sent out foraging expeditions to search for food. He visited local Indians himself and returned with additional food. By the spring of 1609, Newport returned once more, this time with 70 more settlers, including eight Poles and Germans, some of them experts in glassmaking. Newport discovered a revitalized Fort James. A new, freshwater well had been dug and 20 new houses constructed. The number of deaths lessened, and it appeared the colony might survive.

Review and Write

What problems might the colonists have avoided at Fort James had they made wiser decisions?

The Starving Time

By the summer of 1609, many of Fort James's original problems had been addressed. However, despite renewed optimism concerning the future of the colony, the site had proven a deathtrap for hundreds of its earliest colonists. Of the first 300 colonists who arrived in Fort James, only 80 remained alive by the summer of 1609, a survival rate of only one out of four.

Back in England, the merchants of the London Company, heartened by the actions taken by John Smith in reorganizing the colony, set out to repopulate the settlement. They waged a national campaign to recruit new colonists. Their efforts proved successful. Six hundred new settlers signed on to join the colony. By May of 1609, nine ships were readied for the New World.

The voyage proved hazardous and two of the ships were lost, one capsizing in a storm and another wrecked on the island of Bermuda. The remaining seven vessels made their way to Fort James where 400 new colonists arrived in August of 1609.

Once they arrived, they found a colony in disarray. There was little food and housing was scant and inadequate. In addition, they found Captain John Smith wounded from a gunpowder explosion. Without his leadership, the new colonists suffered from their very first day in the New World. (Smith, in fact, had no authority over the new colonists, anyway, according to the new charter they brought with them.) Because of his wounds, Smith left the colony and returned to England.

With the approach of winter, the Jamestown colony began to suffer on a new, more dramatic scale. There was little true leadership or order within the settlement. The new arrivals, many weakened from their transatlantic voyage, never recovered once they arrived and death, once more, was commonplace along the James River.

Life in Jamestown became one of desperation and starvation. Local Indians turned against the village and menaced the inhabitants regularly. They roamed the woods around the village, keeping the settlers trapped inside the walls of the fort. In addition, the natives killed the Jamestown livestock, destroying another food source.

The horrors of that winter of 1609-10, often called "The Starving Time," slowly reduced the number of residents. One colonist wrote of the dreadful experience:

> We were constrained [forced] to eat dogs, cats, rats, snakes, toadstools, horsehides, and what not; one man out of the misery endured, killing his wife, powdered [salted] her up to eat her, for which he was burned. Many besides fed on the corpses of dead men.

One resident became so accustomed to eating human flesh, he developed an appetite for it, and had to be executed by the colonists. By the spring of 1610, the population of Jamestown had been reduced from nearly 500 inhabitants to 60.

Surprisingly, in May, 175 survivors of the Bermuda wreck from the previous summer arrived, having built two small boats from their battered ship. Surveying the situation, both parties of survivors decided to abandon the colony. The party left the rotting fort, bound for England, only to meet at the mouth of the James River, a rescue fleet of ships carrying new colonists and a great store of supplies, food and ammunition. Jamestown had been saved.

Review and Write

1. How did the return of John Smith to England following his wounds from a gunpowder explosion influence the Jamestown colony?

2. What fortunate circumstance saved the Jamestown colony from complete failure?

3. During its first three years, the Jamestown colony experienced ups and downs in its English population. Describe the causes.

Change Comes to Jamestown

Brighter days now lay in store for the inhabitants of the Jamestown colony. Great changes were made in the organization of the colony and new rules of conduct were enacted. While the orders were harsh, calling for the implementation of martial, or military rule, they helped save the colony.

Under the new colonial system, the colonists began to spread out of the Jamestown settlement itself, moving up and down the James River. They built several fortified villages and sowed fields of corn, peas, and barley. So many of the colony's food problems disappeared in time.

The colony also began to see the development of family structures at Jamestown. All the earliest inhabitants to the settlement had been men, but now women began to arrive in increasing numbers. The number of men remained high, however, and men continued to outnumber women for the next several decades. Even by 1650, men outnumbered women at Jamestown by three or four to one. Only by the end of the 17th century did the sex ratio of men to women approach one to one.

One great change at Jamestown was the introduction of a new crop—tobacco. In 1611, one of the Jamestown settlers, John Rolfe, replaced the local variety of tobacco with a type imported from the Caribbean. Europeans had never shown an interest in "Indian tobacco," considering its taste a bit too harsh. When Rolfe also discovered that air-drying helped preserve the full, sweet flavor of the island variety, it helped provide the colony with a much-needed cash crop.

Rolfe experimented with early crops of tobacco and finally exported his first harvest in 1614. Other colonists took up cultivating the short, brown plant and by 1615, a ton of tobacco found its way to England. By 1619, 40,000 pounds were exported. The crop proved so popular and profitable that, by 1629, the colonists of Virginia were exporting 1.5 million pounds of it. At last, the colonists of Virginia had discovered a source of income for their efforts in the New World.

Jamestown residents and other Virginians also experienced a new land policy. Before 1618, all the land occupied by the early colonists at Jamestown belonged to the Virginia Company and had been farmed by the colonists as common land. That year, the company officials agreed to grant 100 acres of land to all colonists who had come to Virginia since 1607. All new colonists were offered 50 acres of land once they paid their passage and had arrived at Jamestown. This system, called the "headright system" put land in the hands of thousands of new immigrants.

One other change took place in Virginia the next year. In 1619, the first elected legislature in America began meeting at Jamestown. The body was called the House of Burgesses, and it was comprised of 22 representatives, or "burgesses," two each elected from the 11 regions of the Virginia colony. Now English government in America consisted of a governor appointed in England who served for life; a council made up of members appointed by the governor, whose duty it was to advise the governor; and an elected legislature. For the first time in the history of the colony, Englishmen were able to pass laws and partially govern themselves.

Review and Write

1. How did the introduction of tobacco and the development of the House of Burgesses change Jamestown?

2. Jamestown struggled during its earliest years and nearly failed to survive as a colony. What later changes helped Jamestown ultimately survive and even prosper as a colonial outpost?

3. John Smith is often described as playing a crucial role in the early history of Jamestown. What important roles did another colonist, John Rolfe, play on behalf of Jamestown's ultimate survival and prosperity?

New Crops, New Labor in Virginia

In many ways, the introduction of tobacco to the colony of Virginia did more to change life in the Tidewater region than anything else. Tobacco growing became a fever, as colonists scrambled for land, even growing the profitable crop in the streets of Jamestown. Not only did tobacco produce a tremendous return of profit, it was also used as a type of money in Virginia. Colonists paid their taxes in tobacco. Public servants, soldiers, even preachers were paid in the profitable brown weed.

For the remainder of the 17th century and through much of the 18th, tobacco was one of the chief exports from the region. By the time of the American Revolution of the 1770s, the colonies were exporting 50 million pounds of tobacco annually. Two colonies dominated the tobacco market in America, Virginia and Maryland.

How profitable was tobacco growing? For one thing, it was a crop which could not be supported in England due to the climate. This meant that English merchants had to import the popular plant. While tobacco was a crop requiring much labor and great attention, the work of one farmer could produce a crop as profitable as the work of six men from an equal number of acres of wheat. Despite the labor involved, tobacco growing did not require much acreage to be profitable. One farmer could raise 1,500 pounds of tobacco annually by only working 1.5 acres of land.

One of the problems with tobacco growing was that the crop wore out the soil quickly. Land cleared for tobacco cultivation could be used for only four to seven years. Because the colonial farmers did not fertilize their lands, tobacco growing sapped the nutrients and minerals from the land, leaving it less productive. This meant that new land had to be found, which caused settlements in the Tidewater to scatter up and down the many rivers of the region.

With the popularity of tobacco in the Tidewater region of Virginia and, later, of Maryland, labor became an important part of the plant's production. A labor shortage developed in Virginia, leading to two new sources of workers. In time, thousands of indentured servants, or contract workers, were imported to the region.

An indentured servant was a colonist too poor to pay his or her passage to America. Instead, a wealthier colonist paid for the voyage, leaving the new arrival with a debt. He or she signed an indenture, obligating him or her to work for their master for a period typically between four and seven years.

During the indenture period, the servant could not marry and, by his or her labor, paid off the debt to the master. At the end of the indenture, the master paid the worker "freedom dues," which often included a suit of clothes, some tools, and seed. Between 1625 and 1640, approximately 1000 indentured servants arrived in the Tidewater each year.

Another group of worker introduced to the English colony at Jamestown were imported Africans. The first arrived on a Dutch ship in Jamestown in 1619. At first, such workers came as indentured servants. The number of blacks in the colony rose slowly. As late as 1671, there were only 2000 of them. But when their status later changed, redefining such workers as "slaves," their numbers increased dramatically.

Review and Write

1. What advantages were there to growing tobacco in the Tidewater region?

2. How did the system of indentured servitude work?

The Calverts Establish Maryland

A generation after English adventurers, backed by London merchants and gentlemen, founded the settlement of Jamestown, Englishmen busied themselves establishing a different kind of colony in North America, just north of the colony of Virginia. It was to be a proprietary colony, and the man responsible for the dream of its creation was an English Catholic named George Calvert.

The Calvert family were loyal supporters of the monarchy, and George was a close friend of King James I. James even granted him a title, bestowing on him the honor of Lord Baltimore. George Calvert even served James as a court official. But when Calvert became a Roman Catholic in 1625, he had to resign his post, for English law stated that only men who were members of the Church of England could hold such positions. Nevertheless, James and Calvert remained good friends.

Since Catholics in England had limited rights in England, George Calvert decided he wanted to establish a colony in the New World. James I granted him land in Newfoundland. But when Calvert and his family attempted a settlement there, it was a failure, due to a poor location.

When James I died in 1625, Charles I came to the throne. As a Catholic supporter (Charles's wife was a Spanish Catholic), Charles, in 1632, granted a new tract of land to Lord Baltimore, this time in the region of the Chesapeake Bay. It was an extensive piece of property which included 10 million acres of land. But George Calvert died suddenly, leaving the grant in question.

Other family members stepped forward and took up the challenge offered by the king's generosity. The grant was reissued to Lord Baltimore's son, Cecilius, who became Lord proprietor of Maryland. The Calverts named their new colony after the queen, Henrietta Maria.

While Cecilius decided to remain in England and administer his colony from a distance, he appointed one of his brothers, Leonard Calvert, to lead the effort to take colonists to the New World.

In December 1633, around 250 would-be colonists boarded two ships, *Dove* and *Ark*, bound for America. The Calverts intended to offer sanctuary to Catholics in their colony. However, they could not advertise such a goal. Nevertheless, about half of his first colonists were Catholics.

The ships arrived in February 1634. The settlers established a settlement they called Saint Mary's. They found the land a rich one, ripe for farming. One colonist wrote: "We cannot go anywhere without stepping on strawberries, raspberries, acorns, walnuts, sassafras, etc."

These first arrivals wasted little time before turning to tobacco planting as their source of livelihood. This helped the colony to begin on a sound footing, allowing the colonists to avoid the problems that had plagued the early years of Jamestown to the south. Other advantages included land that had already been cleared of trees by Indians, who had earlier moved out of the region.

One problem which developed soon in Maryland, however, had to do with religion. Protestants and Catholics sometimes quarreled between themselves. To protect both sides, a law was later passed in Maryland called the Act of Toleration (1649). The law gave all Marylanders the right to worship as they chose.

Review and Write

What advantages gave Marylanders early success in their new colony?

The Spanish Southwest

The English drive to establish colonies in the New World had always been spurred by the success of the Spanish in colonizing the Caribbean and Mexico, as well as South America. Jealous European powers such as England, France, Holland, and others watched great wealth in gold and silver pour into the Spanish capital in Madrid.

During the early 1500s, Spanish explorers and adventurers had trekked across the southern and western portions of the modern-day United States, searching for additional riches. Bold, ruthless conquistadors, including DeSoto and Coronado had also searched for fountains of youth and cities of gold. But these searches were fruitless.

After the great expedition of Coronado across the American Southwest in the 1540s, however, Spain largely abandoned its efforts in the territory that would eventually become the United States. However, a half century later, Spaniards once again ventured north from Mexico. By the 1580s, Franciscan missionaries reentered the region of modern-day New Mexico not in search of great riches, but lost souls.

While the Catholic fathers worked among local Indians, they heard the old stories of great wealth to the north. The Indians told the fathers tales of rich silver and gold mines north of the Rio Grande. As the rumors found their way south to Mexico City, it renewed old Spanish dreams of discovering new wealth, perhaps even another Aztec Empire in the lands they were calling "New Mexico."

In 1598, once again, an intrepid explorer traveled north in search of riches. His name was Juan de Onate, a member of a wealthy mining family. Onate did not travel alone, of course. He brought along 130 soldiers and their families, most of them Indians, as well as 20 missionaries. The expedition numbered around 400 people. Eighty wagons, called carros, carried the party's supplies. Onate provided the monies for the entire expedition.

He moved his party north into the upper Rio Grande Valley of northern New Mexico. There he encountered Pueblo Indians at Acoma, a village situated on a high rock outcropping. The Acoma Pueblo were not friendly to the Spanish, and Onate laid siege to the village. The Acoma natives defended themselves by throwing stones. But eventually, the Spanish reached the Pueblo and slaughtered 800 men, women, and children. The Spanish cut off one foot of each surviving warrior.

Several of those serving under Onate were appalled at his actions taken against the Pueblos. The Indians would never convert to Christianity under such treatment. Some of Onate's party escaped his control and fled. In time, Spanish officials in Mexico City heard of Onate's extreme mistreatment of the Indians, and ordered him to return, stripping him of his titles. (Officials were also disappointed that Onate had not found the fabled gold mines.)

Those who remained behind after Onate's recall established a colony in New Mexico. Their missionaries had some success converting Indians, but the colony did not develop. Then, in 1609, Catholic leaders, excited about the success of New Mexican missionaries, agreed to make New Mexico into a special missionary colony. A new governor arrived in 1610, Don Pedro de Peralta, who founded the capital of Santa Fe, meaning "Holy Faith." This settlement became the first permanent European colony in the American Southwest.

Review and Write

1. What kind of person does Juan de Onate appear to be and what is your opinion of him?

2. After such extensive Spanish explorations as Coronado's across the Southwest, the Spanish abandoned such searches in the lands that would one day be part of the United States. Why did they end such efforts?

3. Within another fifty years, the Spanish had returned to the American Southwest. Why?

Part I.

Matching. *Match the answers shown below with the statements given above. Place the letters of the correct answers in the spaces below.*

1. Italian explorer of 1524 who explored from South Carolina to Newfoundland
2. French naval officer who sailed to America with 150 Huguenots in 1562; founded Charlesfort
3. 1530s French explorer who attempted to build a colony in Canada and failed
4. Spanish colony established in Florida by Menendez de Aviles in summer of 1565
5. Spanish king whose treasure ships were attacked by English "sea dogs"
6. English "sea dog" who circumnavigated the globe in late 1570s
7. English author of book, Discourse of a Discovery for a New Passage to Catia
8. Sailed to Canada in 1576, returned with 1000 tons of fool's gold; he was later lost at sea
9. Half brother to Humphrey Gilbert, he attempted to establish English colony on Roanoke Island
10. English artist who sketched pictures of Native Americans he encountered at Roanoke
11. First English child born in the New World
12. Leader of 1606 English attempt to colonize along Maine coast near Kennebec River

A. Cartier	B. Philip II	C. Humphrey Gilbert	D. Walter Raleigh
E. Verrazano	F. Martin Frobisher	G. Martin Pring	H. Virginia Dare
I. Jean Ribaut	J. St. Augustine	K. Francis Drake	L. John White

1. ____ 2. ____ 3. ____ 4. ____ 5. ____ 6. ____ 7. ____ 8. ____ 9. ____ 10. ____ 11. ____ 12. ____

Part II.

Matching. *Match the answers shown below with the statements given above. Place the letters of the correct answers in the spaces below.*

1. Sea captain who guided three English ships to Virginia in 1607 to establish colony
2. Monarch for whom the English colonial settlement in Virginia was named in 1607
3. Military captain who helped organize Jamestown colonists, ordering them to work for food
4. Local Indian alliance that attacked the Jamestown settlement early after its establishment
5. Introduced tobacco type to Jamestown colony which soon developed into serious cash crop
6. Land distribution system established in Tidewater region, granted 50 acres per person
7. Colonial assembly created in 1619 which was first elected legislature in America
8. Type of servant imported to America who was bound to work for five to 7 years
9. English monarch who chartered the colony of Maryland
10. Catholic family who received the charter for Maryland
11. Maryland law which granted right to worship as one pleased
12. Spanish governor who, in 1610, founded the capital of Santa Fe in the Southwest

A. John Smith	B. headright	C. Calverts	D. Act of Toleration
E. James I	F. John Rolfe	G. indentured	H. House of Burgesses
I. De Peralta	J. Powhatan	K. Charles I	L. Newport

1. ____ 2. ____ 3. ____ 4. ____ 5. ____ 6. ____ 7. ____ 8. ____ 9. ____ 10. ____ 11. ____ 12. ____

Champlain's New France

French attempts to establish colonies along the Atlantic seaboard of the modern-day United States had proven unsuccessful in the late 1500s. After the Spanish destruction of the French settlement at Fort Caroline in the 1560s, the French abandoned its efforts in the region. All later efforts to colonize were centered on Canada.

One great French explorer and colonizer led the way in the renewed effort to establish a permanent French presence in the New World. Samuel de Champlain was destined to become the founder of New France.

Champlain was born in 1567 in a small seaport town on the Brittany peninsula. He served as a French soldier and helped drive the Spanish out of France. The young Champlain then went to Spain in 1598, and later sailed to the New World with an uncle. They traveled throughout the Caribbean for the next three years, visiting Cuba, Mexico, and Panama.

In 1603, he joined a French fleet bound for Canada, intending to establish a trading colony along the Saint Lawrence River. At the former site of an Indian village called "Stadacone," the French established their post called *Kebec* after an Indian word meaning "where the river narrows."

Champlain brought unique skills to the New World. Not only was he a seasoned soldier, he was also a writer, artist, and mapmaker. On his first trip to Canada, he remained in Canada for only three months. During that time, he made friends with local Indians, including the Algonquians. His friendship with these Native Americans would prove invaluable in the settling of Canada by the French. Champlain heard remarkable stories from the Algonquians about the Great Lakes to the west and of Niagara Falls. Few Europeans had ever heard of these significant landforms.

Champlain returned to France and began writing about his adventures in Canada. He was certain that France could establish a great series of colonies in North America. Champlain soon became an accepted authority about the Canadian north. In 1604, when Pierre du Guast, the Sieur de Monts, made a trip to Canada, Champlain was certain to be among his party. De Monts brought three ships and 120 men, intending to establish a year-round trading post. He also wanted to provide a place for French people to practice the religion of their choice. The group arrived in May 1604.

After De Monts' party spent a horrific winter on the Bay of Fundy on the Atlantic Coast, where 35 members of the group died, they moved on to Port Royal on the island of Nova Scotia (now Annapolis Royal). Champlain again returned to France in 1607. His days of following others in the New World were over. When De Monts received permission from the French king to establish a second trading post in Canada, Champlain agreed to lead the new party into the wilderness.

In the spring of 1608, Champlain returned to Canada and established a trading post on the Saint Lawrence at Kebec, which was by then called "Quebec." This post proved extremely successful and Quebec soon became the center of the French fur trade in North America. But Champlain still faced many adventures in the years ahead.

Review and Write

Why were French efforts to colonize Canada more successful than their efforts to colonize southern sites such as Fort Caroline?

Native Americans and New France

One key to the success of Champlain's efforts in helping to colonize Canada for the French was his understanding of the Native Americans. He believed the French would never succeed in North America without help from the Native Americans. Since profitable trade in the New World colony of Quebec, for example, depended on Indian involvement, Champlain's desire for strong ties between the French and the Native Americans was well founded.

But allying with one or another group of Indians in Canada automatically placed the French on opposite sides with other tribes who were often already traditional enemies of tribes friendly to the French trappers and traders. Champlain discovered this to be true when he sided with the Algonquian tribes of the Huron and the Algonquians against their enemies, the Haudenosaunee. (The Algonquians called them *Iroquois* meaning "terrible people.")

When his fur-trading Indian partners formed a war party against the Haudenosaunee, Champlain joined them. During a battle with a Haudenosaunee tribe known as the Mohawk, Champlain and his men used their firearms, called *arquebuses*, against them. This was one of the first times Canadian Indians had seen the use of these early muskets. The natives would come to call them "thunder horns."

During the raid, Champlain's men killed three Haudenosaunee chiefs. This small battle also set the course for Indian alliances in Canada and North America for the next century. The Iroquois, remembering Champlain's involvement, would later ally themselves with the English. From that year on, Indian warfare would include firearms.

Over the next several years, Champlain worked hard to consolidate French power in Canada. Through diplomacy, he negotiated trade treaties with many tribes of Native Americans. He dispatched trade agents and French traders to live with the Indians, instructing them to learn the native practices, customs, and languages. The fur trade in Canada soon became extremely profitable.

But Champlain always considered Quebec, the center of the French presence in Canada, the first step in New World colonial expansion. He made plans to go "inland as far as the Western Sea [the Pacific Ocean], and . . . later even reach China." When Indians told him of great bodies of water to the west, Champlain went and explored, finding the Great Lakes of Ontario and Huron.

Despite the success of "New France," the French colonies of Canada were always underpopulated. The French government encouraged families to settle in Acadia along the shores of the Bay of Fundy and along the fertile Saint Lawrence River, but few came over. Those who did became "inhabitants," farmers, working the lands of "seigneurs," or wealthier, land-owning men. Small settlements developed, typically including a manor house for the landowning lord, a Catholic church, and a public building, patterned after those found in northern France. Using Indian farming methods, the inhabitants were able to produce crops despite a short growing season.

While such an arrangement of settlement helped to expand the New World economy for the French, the backbone of New France remained the trappers and traders who ventured along rivers and lakes in search of beaver pelts.

Review and Write

1. Describe the development of New France into a productive colony.

2. Champlain would prove himself to be one of the most successful of France's colonizers in the New World. What were the secrets of Champlain's ability to succeed in the New World where others failed?

3. What effect did the alliance of Champlain's men with the Algonquians in a battle against the Mohawks have on the future of French-Indian relations in Canada?

A French Empire Built on Fur

Without the success of the fur trade between the French and their native allies in Canada, New France would probably not have become a permanent presence in North America. Thousands of brave, intrepid Frenchmen participated in the trade, negotiating with Indians for furs and often trapping beaver themselves.

The fur trade itself, in fact, would not have been nearly as profitable as it was in the 17th and 18th centuries had beaver not become such a fashionable material to wear in Europe. During these years, the wearing of beaver was extremely popular in both France and England. Fashionable men wore beaver hats and stylish women wore beaver coats and capes. Beaver became the rage among the wealthy in Paris and London, and later in Quebec and Montreal.

To the Native Americans who traded with the French, it was all very strange. They did not understand how popular beaver was to the wealthy people of Europe. One Algonquian native spoke for many of his brothers when, in 1634, he said: "They [Europeans] have no sense; they give us twenty knives for one beaver skin." The trade was profitable for both sides.

With each passing decade, the French trappers became familiar with more and more territory to the west of Quebec. They learned the locations of rivers, forests, and lakes, discovering the best routes to take them further into the interior. As French trappers reached new territory, forts were often erected to provide trade centers.

Two general types of French trappers soon developed. The *coureurs de bois* (KOO-rurz day-BWAH) hunted and traded in the forest regions of Canada. The *voyageurs* (VWAH-jurz) traveled further west out onto the Canadian Plains. There were many similarities between the two types. Both groups often married Indian women, which helped them become friends to various tribes. The Frenchmen usually treated their Indian partners with respect and avoided cheating them. As these men traveled further west, they were able to claim additional land as part of New France.

One of the first of the coureurs de bois was a young Quebec colonist named Etienne Brule. Champlain employed him to go west and negotiate for trade with the Huron. Brule explored extensively throughout eastern Canada, and even trekked as far south as the Chesapeake Bay, making him one of the first Europeans to reach modern-day Pennsylvania. (Brule was later killed after a dispute with the Huron.)

The work of the French trappers, traders, and explorers was difficult and hazardous. They often worked in extreme cold, risking death at the hands of unfriendly Indians. But it could be exciting work, too.

The high point of each year's trading and trapping season came in the spring, when the coureurs de bois fanned out across the forests north of the Great Lakes, making renewed contact with their Indian trading partners. The Indians spent the winter trapping beaver and accumulating animal pelts. Near the region of Michilimackinac and Green Bay, north of Lake Michigan, the French and Indians gathered, the Indian canoes filled with packs of beaver hides.

They formed a great fleet of hundreds of canoes which then began the trip toward Montreal, founded as a trading city in 1642. There the governor of Quebec greeted the flotilla, wearing a scarlet cloak. He then sat down with the natives and smoked with them, reminding them of their friendship.

Review and Write

1. What were the basic differences between coureurs de bois and voyageurs?

2. Why and how were the French able to base their New World efforts on fur trading?

3. What contributions did French trappers make to the French effort to expand its influence across Canada?

The Voyage of Marquette and Joliet

As the French expanded their presence across Canada and beyond the Great Lakes, the significance of the French colonial efforts became unmistakable. Their rewards did not come in the form of vast accumulations of gold and silver as with the Spanish far to the south. Their's was a colony based on hard work, determination, and friendly relations with Indians based on mutual trade. (The Spanish, on the other hand, enslaved the native populations of the Caribbean, Mexico, and South America.)

In 1661, a new king came to the throne in France. He was Louis XIV, and he was to become the greatest king in the history of his nation. For decades Louis ruled, determined that France would be the most powerful country in Europe. Before he died in 1715, the French army numbered a half million men, the French economy was dominant around the world, and his nation was a leader in the arts and in fashion.

Part of Louis's plan to expand French power worldwide was to build up his nation's holdings in the New World. He appointed a new Intendant of New France named Jean Talon. It became Talon's task to expand the French presence and increase the income from the fur trade.

As part of Talon's plan of expansion, he relied on the traveling missionaries known as Jesuits. The black-robed priests, by the 1670s, were concentrating their efforts in the region of land where Lakes Michigan, Huron, and Superior come together. Natives told the priests stories of a great river to the south called the Mississippi.

In 1672, Talon dispatched two men, a French trader named Louis Joliet and a Jesuit priest, Father Jacques Marquette, to make a reconnaissance south of the Great Lakes in search of the great river reported by Indians. Before they finished their journey of exploration, the two men had traveled 2,500 miles together.

The two men chosen for the expedition were exactly the ones needed. Marquette was extremely popular with the Great Lakes tribes he encountered. And Joliet was a mapmaker, as well as a trader. He

was also a fearless man, who would push on in the face of crushing odds.

The party actually set out in search of the Mississippi River in 1673. They traveled in birchbark canoes along with five other Frenchmen and two Indians who served as guides. The men journeyed from Quebec and followed the Ottawa River to the west. Along the way they made contact at French forts where they received information and supplies. From Fort Michilimackinac they floated to Green Bay, then portaged (meaning they carried their canoes) between the Fox and Wisconsin Rivers until they reached the Mississippi River, at a site located today in the state of Wisconsin. On June 17, 1673, Father Marquette wrote in his journal, "we safely entered the Mississippi."

Down the river they paddled, meeting new Indian tribes along the way. From the Illinois Indians, Father Marquette received a peace pipe which he used as a "passport" when they encountered other tribes further south. Some Indians, including the Shawnee, warned the Frenchmen that further south they would encounter the Spanish.

Taking such warning seriously, Marquette and Joliet floated as far south as the site where the Arkansas River flows into the Mississippi. Here they turned back and headed north again. Based on their travels, the two explorers claimed the entire region of the Mississippi River Valley for France.

Review and Write

What significance did the voyage of Joliet and Father Marquette hold for France?

LaSalle's Explorations

The return trip for the intrepid trader and his priest friend was a difficult one. They traveled upriver until they reached the Illinois River (just north of modern-day St. Louis, Missouri) and returned by a different route than they had taken originally, following the Great Lakes back to Quebec.

When Joliet and Marquette reported back to French authorities in Quebec, they had valuable information about the lands they had explored and claimed for France. They relayed Indian stories about the lower reaches of the Mississippi, telling their superiors that the river flows into the Gulf of Mexico. While the news brought back to Quebec was well-received, the French did not immediately follow up on it.

But in time, others followed in their footsteps. Nearly a decade after their voyage, a Frenchman named René Robert Cavelier, Sieur de La Salle, prepared a party to explore further the region traversed by Marquette and Joliet. The time was right for his expedition. The French were, for the time being, at peace with the Haudenosaunee, which would allow them to explore without any real threat from the traditional enemies of the French.

In January of 1682, La Salle set out with 54 men to further explore the Mississippi River Valley. Among his men were 31 Indians. In some ways, La Salle saw himself as a French version of the Spanish conquistador Cortés. He was bold and energetic, but he was also a haughty man who often became impatient with others. He was not an easy man to like.

La Salle's first plan was to sail the Mississippi River in a ship weighing 40 tons. Such a large vessel would not have been easy to transport or portage between rivers. Luckily, La Salle grew impatient and left with his men before the ship's completion. Instead, La Salle utilized canoes just as Marquette and Joliet had.

La Salle's party established forts along their voyage, including Fort Crèvecoeur. This settlement was the first established by white men in the present-day state of Illinois. (On the return trip, they erected Fort Saint Louis along the Illinois River.) Before he was finished, La Salle and his party floated south to the mouth of the Mississippi where they viewed the great waters of the Gulf of Mexico. La Salle claimed the entire region for France, naming it Louisiana, after the French king, Louis XIV.

La Salle now set out to solidify the French presence in the Mississippi River Valley. He returned to France, where he raised the funds to establish a colony near the mouth of the great American river. In 1684, he returned to the Gulf of Mexico with 200 would-be colonists aboard four ships, filled with supplies and equipment for their New World venture.

But, in searching for the mouth of the Mississippi, La Salle mistakenly identified Matagorda Bay, in Texas, as the river's end. When his party landed, they were besieged by Indians. Soon, La Salle realized his error and proceeded east on foot in search of the true location of the Mississippi. While searching, some of his party turned on the leader they no longer believed in, and killed La Salle. Those remaining in the fledgling colony struggled until they abandoned the colony altogether. Miraculously, some of the survivors followed the Mississippi River, returning to Quebec on foot.

Review and Write

1   The two explorers, Father Marquette and Louis Joliet returned from their voyage of discovery and provided what information to French authorities about the New World?

2. Who was the Frenchman, René Robert Cavelier, Sieur de La Salle, and what was his connection to the voyage of Marquette and Joliet?

3. As LaSalle attempted to establish a French colony in the Mississippi River Valley, what mistakes did he make that doomed the success of the French venture in the Gulf of Mexico?

                    © Milliken Publishing Company

Hudson Sails for the Dutch

While large and powerful nation states such as France and Spain flexed their muscles in the New World, even smaller, less dominant countries also became involved in the European exploration of the Americas. One such country was Holland.

Prior to 1566, the people of Holland—known as the Dutch—were dominated by the Spanish. The Spanish king ruled their country and imposed higher and higher taxes on them. Protestants in Holland were also persecuted. Once the Dutch successfully revolted against their Spanish oppressors, they too were free to expand their trade and shipping around the world.

Under the Dutch Republic, the merchants, shippers, and traders of Holland established trade connections from Africa to Russia, and from the Mediterranean to the Spice Islands of the Far East. Dutch trading vessels sailed to the New World, and established settlements in South America and a few of the Caribbean Islands.

One of the largest Dutch trading companies formed during this period was the East India Company, established in 1602. Primarily involved in spice trade, the company proved to be a formidable rival of other European trading nations in the region, especially the Spanish and Portuguese.

In an attempt to avoid shipping lanes which put Dutch ships in the path of their trade rivals in the Far East, the Dutch East India Company offered a cash prize to any sea captain who could discover a western route through the New World to the Orient. An English pilot named Henry Hudson took up the challenge.

In January 1609, Hudson contracted with the Dutch East India Company to sail to America in search of the long elusive Northwest Passage. Onboard a company ship, the *Half Moon*, Hudson organized a crew of Dutch and English sailors. During the voyage across the Atlantic, his crew came to realize that Hudson was a stubborn, fussy man, but a highly skilled mariner. Despite threatening storms, Hudson landed his ship at Newfoundland in the summer of 1609. After the crew fished for cod in the region, Hudson pressed on, exploring the coast of Maine, where the *Half Moon* hosted a canoe full of Penobscot Indians.

Hudson pushed on, intent on his goal and the prize money. He sailed to Virginia then turned north, sailing back into Canadian water, landing at the mouth of a river in modern-day New York City. Today, that river is known as the Hudson River. He sailed up the Hudson to the site of present-day Albany, but when the river narrowed, he knew he was following a false lead. Hudson noted several sites along the river that could serve as Dutch colonies or trading posts. Soon, the Dutch would establish a presence in the New World, at a site which they would call New Netherland.

Hudson returned to England and dispatched a report to officials of the Dutch East India Company. When the English king, James I, realized that Hudson had just completed a voyage of discovery for the Dutch, Hudson was arrested and tossed into jail. For Hudson, things looked bleak for awhile, until a group of English merchants decided that the errant English sea captain could serve them as a New World mariner.

They hired Hudson to work for them (the *Half Moon* had already been delivered by his crew back to the Dutch East India Company). Hudson signed a new contract, this time with his native Englishmen, to sail to the Canadian region of Labrador in search of a route that would allow English traders to steer clear of French fur posts on the St. Lawrence River.

As Hudson began preparing for his next voyage to North America, he could not know it was to be his last.

Review and Write

What was the historical connection between the Dutch and the Spanish before 1566, and how did that relationship change later in the 16th century?

The Dutch Found New Netherland

Henry Hudson, now in the employ of the English, set sail for the New World once again in 1610. When he and his crew reached Canada, they sailed north to steer clear of the French settlements and trading posts. Hudson entered a strait which is today named for him. This route gave him access to a great, expansive inland bay which would also be named for the explorer.

The intrepid explorer sailed his ship along the east coast of Hudson Bay to its southern end, probably close to where James Bay is today. It was to be a dreadful experience. Winter set in hard, leaving the ship locked in the ice of the bay.

When the ship finally broke free, Hudson insisted they continue their explorations. Tired of Hudson's difficult ways and arrogant disposition, the crew turned on Hudson, mutinied, tossing the captain, his young son, and a handful of sailors loyal to Hudson into one of the ship's small boats, providing them with no food or other provisions. The mutineers left them in the bay and sailed back to England. When word was received at home of the mutiny against Hudson, a rescue ship was sent in search of him and his fellow crewmen. However, no trace of the men was ever found, and Hudson's fate remains a mystery.

While Hudson had failed to find the Northwest Passage, his explorations proved valuable to both the English and the Dutch in later years. More than a half century later, the English followed up Hudson's voyage by returning to the great bay that bears his name, establishing a fur trading company, also named for the lost explorer, the Hudson Bay Company. The profits from such trade were immediate and this great trading company would continue as a great English and Canadian enterprise for hundreds of years.

But what of the Dutch? They too followed up Hudson's explorations in the Americas. Wasting no time, the Dutch returned to the region of New York, sailed up the Hudson River, and established a trading post on an island near today's Albany, which they called Fort Orange, named for a royal family in Holland.

Fort Orange was only the first of a series of trading posts and forts to be established by the Dutch. They also built settlements at the mouth of the Delaware River, along the Hudson River, and on the southern tip of an island occupied by the Manhatta Indians. (Of course, today it is known as Manhattan Island.) This new colonial system of posts was called New Netherland.

Less than a decade later, in 1621, Dutch merchants established a new company called the Dutch West India Company. While the company had outposts in Brazil and engaged in the West African slave trade, they put much energy and effort into New Netherland, as well. Settlers were encouraged, and in 1623, the company brought over its first emigrants, settling them on Manahatta. Over the next two years, the New Amsterdam Dutch built a fort, a windmill, and a protective wall marking the town of New Amsterdam. (Today's "Wall Street" in New York City is this Dutch wall.) In 1626, the colony received its first governor, Peter Minuit, who "purchased" the entire island from a local Indian clan for 60 guilders (about $24 dollars equivalent). The Dutch presence in North America seemed firmly established.

Review and Write

How did the voyages of Henry Hudson help the English and Dutch to establish posts in the New World?

The Story of the Puritans

Their story is one of the first history lessons American school children hear. Elementary school bulletin boards present them as a funnily-dressed man and woman wearing black and white clothes—she in a long, plain dress and white cap, and he sporting a black coat, pants, and hat, with white stockings and black shoes with big gold buckles.

Most American students know them as the Pilgrims and their story involves November, eating turkey, and the first Thanksgiving. But there is much more to the story of the founding of the English colonies in the region they would come to call "New England."

It is true that the people who would settle New England were quite different from those who founded settlements in Virginia. While they came to America for some of the same reasons as did other English men and women, the founders of New England were also seeking religious freedom.

The story of the Puritans began just after the 1534 separation of England from the Roman Catholic Church. King Henry VIII, for both personal and national reasons, allowed the development of a separate Christian church, called the Church of England, with himself as its head. This movement away from Catholicism encouraged other Christians, called Protestants, to develop their own religious ideas and institutions.

The Puritans were among the Protestants. They hoped to one day change the Church of England, to make it less formal. They wished to "purify" the church. Puritans did not support the idea of an official priesthood, and wanted to practice a religion that allowed them to interpret the Bible as they saw fit.

Not only did the Puritans desire less formality in church, they also sought to live their lives more simply, without involvement in the distractions of the world. They believed that activities such as dancing or attending the theater were sinful and should be avoided. Instead, they tried to fill their lives with honest work, which they said gave them all the happiness they would need in this world.

The Puritans began to believe that the Church of England would never be "purified," and began to separate themselves from it completely, calling themselves Separatists. From time to time, Separatists were punished for their beliefs, since the English monarchy gave its support to the Church of England.

One group of Separatists lived in Scrooby, England. They became dissatisfied with life in England, and decided to leave their native home and sail to Holland where they knew they would not be persecuted for their faith. But life in the Dutch city of Leyden did not satisfy the Separatists. They were free to practice their religion as they wanted, but the people of the city were more worldly in the eyes of the Separatists than were their fellow Englishmen. They also found jobs scarce.

Some Separatist leaders began to talk of establishing a new home for themselves in America, a place where they could practice their religious beliefs—a land that would serve as their "new" England.

Review and Write

1. The story of the Pilgrims is well known to American school children. How do young students visualize the Pilgrims?

2. What did the terms "Puritan" and "Separatist" refer to as they relate to the Church of England?

3. The first European colonizers of New England were known religiously as the Puritans. What was Puritanism and how did its advocates look at the Church of England?

4. From the Puritans, another group developed, called the Separatists. How were the Separatists different from the Puritans?

Seeking a Place to Worship

As the dream of a Puritan settlement in the New World began to take root, the Separatists enlisted help from none other than Captain John Smith. Smith had returned to England from Jamestown after suffering severe wounds from a gunpowder explosion in 1609. After his recovery, the Virginia Company of London refused to rehire him. Instead, Smith signed on in 1614 as a captain of a small whaling fleet bound for America. The whaling operation set up base along the coast of what Smith would later call "New England."

While there, John Smith explored the region, surveyed it, and drew detailed maps. He came to believe it would make a good site for an English colony. When he published his work in a book titled *A Description of New England* (1617), Smith described the land in glowing terms, imagining a place:

> *planted with gardens and corn fields, and so well inhabited with a goodly, strong and well proportioned people [Native Americans] besides the greatness of the timber growing on them, the greatness of the fish and the moderate temper of the year. Who can but approve this a most excellent place, both for health and fertility?*

John Smith's book would serve as a part of the developing Puritan dream of migrating to the New World and building a community of people with similar beliefs. Two of the Scrooby sect's leaders, William Brewster and William Bradford, read Smith's book with great enthusiasm.

When life in Holland proved less than satisfactory, the Separatists began looking for an opportunity elsewhere. It came in 1620. For three years, Puritan leaders had negotiated with the Dutch for a settlement site in New Netherland. When efforts failed, the Puritans decided to tie themselves to the Virginia Company of Plymouth, their fellow Englishmen. They contracted with company officials, promising to build a colony, living together on common lands, and sending the profits from their labor and trade with local Indians back to the company's investors. But under the agreement, the Puritans were supposed to establish their colony in Virginia, not John Smith's New England.

On August 15, 1620, the Puritans, who now saw themselves as pilgrims—a people traveling to an unknown, foreign land—sailed from Holland back to England in a ship known as the *Speedwell*, an old vessel badly in need of repair. Once they arrived in England, the party was joined by other Separatists, as well as additional Englishmen, whom the Separatists called "strangers," looking for a chance to go to America. A second ship was to be included in the transatlantic voyage, an old, wine vessel known as the *Mayflower*.

When the Pilgrims realized the *Speedwell* would not seaworthy enough to complete the trip to America, the decision was made to sail on the *Mayflower* alone. In September, 1620, the party of 102 passengers, Puritans and strangers, including men, women, and children, set a course for America.

Review and Write

1. In what ways did the founding of the Jamestown colony lead to the Puritans' plans to establish a place for themselves in the New World?

2. Although Captain John Smith first came to America to help the Jamestown colony, he later returned to America and helped the Puritans in their colony. What contributions did he make to the New England colonizing efforts?

3. In 1617, John Smith published a book called *A Description of New England*. What impact did the book have on the founding of the New World colony of the Puritans?

4. As the religious group of Separatists began planning their new colony in the New World, how did they envision their settlement?

25

The Pilgrims Land in America

The voyage on the *Mayflower* proved to be one of hardship and danger. The people onboard were crowded together and had few comforts. Children and others grew seasick. Some of the sailors, themselves worldly men, occasionally taunted the highly religious Pilgrims.

Because they were largely poor people, the trip was underfinanced. The *Mayflower* was an older vessel, not intended for passengers. The water onboard soured, and the ale went stale. Their food molded, and the flour barrels were soon full of maggots and weevils. The *Mayflower* was soon a ship of great misery.

The party was bound for Virginia when they left England. But violent storms blew them to the north, keeping them off course. In one hurricane, the main beam below decks on the *Mayflower* shattered in two, crippling the vessel, seeming to spell certain disaster. The ship seemed as though it would break apart, with water quickly pouring in. But the Pilgrims thought fast and used one of their jacks, meant to raise their houses in America, to force the splintered beam back into position.

The Pilgrims faced little death on their trip to America. One person died, but another was born, a baby who was appropriately named Oceanus. For 66 days, the party faced rough seas until the *Mayflower* came in sight of land. But they were not in Virginia. The storms and constant winds had driven the small ship to the very place the Pilgrims had read about in John Smith's book, New England. Specifically, they dropped anchor off Cape Cod, a long neck of land which today is part of Massachusetts. The date for their landing in the New World was November 21, 1620. (Under the calendar in use at that time, the date was actually November 11.)

Questions immediately rose about what steps to take next. Should the party attempt to sail down the coast to Virginia or remain where they were? They knew it was late in the season, and that winter was coming on. The leaders among the Pilgrims decided to remain at Cape Cod.

But the Pilgrims' contract did not give them the right to settle in New England. They had no authority to be there or to establish a colony there. Such questions about authority led the party to create an agreement among themselves called the Mayflower Compact. Forty-one male adults signed the document onboard the *Mayflower*. The purpose of the compact was to create a contract among the colonists in which they agreed to govern themselves and accept the decisions of the leaders. The Mayflower Compact is one of the first examples of a document recognizing self-government in North America. Under the agreement, the men elected John Carver as their first governor.

Over several weeks, the Pilgrims explored the coast around Cape Cod Bay. At a site they later called Plymouth, the colonists found an abandoned Indian village, which had been struck by a smallpox epidemic a few years earlier. The site offered cleared land, a freshwater stream, and was situated on top of a hill which could be easily defended. On December 26, the Pilgrims anchored the *Mayflower* at Plymouth. Despite the prayers of the Puritans, no one knew exactly what lay ahead for the weary colonists.

Review and Write

Why was the Mayflower Compact such a unique document?

The Indians Provide Support

Having arrived too late in the New World to plant crops, the Pilgrims experienced food shortages and malnutrition during their first winter. Already weakened by a terrible voyage, the colonists became ill, probably from scurvy, a disease caused by vitamin deficiencies. Ironically, the Pilgrims were living close to cranberry bogs and cranberries are a fruit high in vitamin C, a sure cure for scurvy.

Half of these early settlers at Plymouth died during their first winter. Just as earlier colonies, such as Jamestown and Roanoke had been rescued from extinction with help from local Indians, so too, the Pilgrims received assistance from a Native American named Massasoit. He was the sachem, or leader, of the tribe called the Wampanoags. While Massasoit offered the Pilgrims food, including Indian corn, he also wanted to ally with the English against a tribal enemy, the Narragansets.

The language barrier between the English at Plymouth and the Indians might have been more difficult, except for a Native American who served as an interpreter. His name was Squanto, and much to the surprise of the Pilgrims, he spoke English. Squanto had just returned to New England a year earlier after having spent years away.

Squanto had been taken on an English fishing vessel to England in 1605. He lived there until 1614, spending several years in London. In 1614, he was returned to his native land, but was later that same year kidnapped by a English sea captain and sold in Spain as a slave. In time, he escaped and returned to England, only to be returned once more to New England in 1619. On his return, he found his village of Pawtuxet Indians had been wiped out by a plague.

With no place to go, Squanto had joined the Wampanoags, serving as an adviser and interpreter for Massasoit. Squanto taught the Pilgrims how to live off the New England landscape, giving them instruction where to fish and how to plant Indian corn.

The settlers of Plymouth Plantation struggled during these early years to carve a colony out of the harsh New England landscape. Among those who died that first winter was John Carver, the first elected governor of the settlement. Governor William Bradford, a Puritan elder, took his place and provided solid leadership for the young settlement. But even after the deadly first winter of 1621, the colonists continued to face significant problems.

Since they had landed far north of their original land grant, the Pilgrims had to obtain a legitimate grant, or patent. Also, they had contracted a heavy debt to their wealthy English backers and it took the colonists several years of hard labor to pay off that obligation. Mostly they did so by shipping furs and fish back to England.

Peace with the local Indians remained important to the Pilgrims, and they worked hard to maintain good relations with their Native American neighbors. They did train for war, relying heavily on the skills of their only professional soldier, Miles Standish. But Indian attack was not a problem during the first years at Plymouth. Squanto, living on a small plot of land in the Pilgrim settlement, was able to help maintain the peace, until he died in 1622.

While the early years at Plymouth were spent living communally, it did not take long before new settlers arrived and scattered out, establishing a town settlement pattern. Slowly, the Plymouth colony developed into a viable settlement with an ever-increasing population.

Review and Write

1. What important roles did Native Americans play in helping the Pilgrims through their first winter at Plymouth?

2. When the English Separatists arrived at Plymouth, they discovered a Native American named Squanto who spoke English. Describe the adventures of Squanto that gave him a knowledge of English.

The Puritan "Great Migration"

Less than a decade after the founding of the Plymouth colony by the Puritans, along with others the Puritans called "strangers," a great influx of new colonists found their way to New England, which changed English life there dramatically.

In 1625, Charles I came to the throne of England. He despised the Puritans, many of whom were members of Parliament. He sent agents out to persecute them, breaking up their meetings and harassing their leaders. So, in 1629, John Winthrop, a Puritan lawyer, decided he and his fellow believers could find a better life in America. He organized a group of would-be Puritan emigrants, eager to go to New England.

The previous year, the Council for New England, the ruling Puritan body in Plymouth, granted a group of Puritans a patent on some land located between the Merrimack and Charles Rivers, north of Plymouth. It was John Winthrop's group that obtained the charter to set up a royal colony there in 1629.

The next year, 1630, the Massachusetts Bay Company was formed. It took its name from a local Indian tribe, which meant "near the great hill." The company organized recruitments to New England, and in March, 11 ships carrying more than 1000 emigrants left for America. This was the largest group of settlers that had ever left Europe, landing on June 12, 1630, at a site they called Salem.

John Winthrop was one of the group's leaders. After the arrival of the "Great Migration," he became the first governor of the Massachusetts Bay colony. Despite the group's high hopes, they faced immediate disappointment when they arrived. The organizers of the Massachusetts Bay Company had sent a small group of advance colonists ahead of the main migration group to help prepare the site for the later arrivals. When the ships of the Great Migration arrived, they found one out of every four of the advance group had already died. This frightened some, and 200 of the new settlers decided to return back to England rather than risk their lives in America. Governor Winthrop knew the key

to his colony's survival lay in the delivery of much needed supplies and food to Salem from England.

One of the 11 ships of the Great Migration, the *Lyon*, returned to England with Winthrop's order for such supplies. But before the *Lyon* could return, 200 settlers died in the Massachusetts Bay colony. Many of those who had survived had contracted scurvy. Onboard the *Lyon*, which returned in February 1631, however, was the cure: a large quantity of lemons.

That first winter of 1630-31 proved to be a difficult one. But the settlers worked hard, building shelters. One of the first structures Winthrop ordered built was the Puritan meetinghouse, for worship. Some help came to the Massachusetts immigrants from Plymouth. Indian corn, clams, and seafood were the foods the colonists came to rely on.

Salem proved to be an inadequate location to support a large community early on, so Winthrop moved many of his people south to a site which was named Charlestown. But there, also, problems arose. The water supply was not enough to support the large group, so Winthrop moved them again, to a place nearby named Boston. This location proved suitable, and Boston soon became the main town of the colony.

Review and Write

How did John Winthrop show good leadership over the Massachusetts Bay colony?

The New England Way

With each passing decade of the 1600s, the English presence in New England became one more settled and less risky to new inhabitants. And more inhabitants were coming all the time. Between 1629 and 1643, 20,000 new arrivals reached New England. Boston became the center of a beehive of colonization, as settlements fanned out to a distance of 30 miles away.

What developed was the "New England Way," a lifestyle and pattern of settlement which might resemble that of life in England itself, but unique to its American home. The first houses erected by the Puritans were nearly identical to those they had lived in before migrating—a wooden house with a single room, the outer walls covered with clay daub mixed with animal dung. These "daub and wattle" homes were roofed with bundles of reeds or thatch and were similar to those built by other English colonists in places such as Jamestown.

In time, as prosperity came to the colonies of the Puritans, they built larger homes, usually two-story, featuring clapboard siding. The well-known saltbox house of the 1600s was noted for roofs steeper on one side than the other, as a preventive to heavy snow accumulation. The homes of the prosperous sported gables, with window boxes that extended out from the line of the roof.

Typical second-generation New England houses had small windows and an entry door centered along the front side of the dwelling. The first floor included a staircase positioned at the front entrance of the house, with a centrally located fireplace that provided the indoor heat source and the means for cooking meals.

The first floor was often divided into four rooms including a sitting room (also known as "the best room"), a front room similar to modern-day living rooms, a kitchen and dining room at the rear of the house, and finally, a spare room which provided a bedroom for a servant or could be used for storage. Since the windows were small and few, the interior was often dark. (Window openings were minimal because glass was expensive.)

The upstairs portion of the home was often divided into two bedrooms. All the rooms in the house would typically have only a few pieces of furniture. The kitchen, for example, might feature a long wooden table where the entire family could eat a meal together. (The younger children did not sit at the table, however, but had to stand during the entire meal.) Utensils and food service would be just the essentials. Most people in early New England ate from wooden bowls or platters called trenchers, using wooden spoons. Forks were uncommon. Kitchen utensils included pots, pans, butter churns, kettles, skillets, roasting spits, and an earlier form of the toaster: a wrought iron rack that could be turned to toast both sides of the food being heated.

Family life was always important in the development of the New England settlements, villages, and towns. Many of the immigrants to Massachusetts came as families that might include not only a father, mother, and children (often as many as five to eight), but a grandmother and/or grandfather, as well. With so many children in New England, many schools were established.

Such extended families produced significant social differences in New England. Typically, people in New England lived longer, had more children, and were healthier than those living in other 17th-century settlements.

Review and Write

1. How were colonial, Puritan houses practical places to live?

2. Between 1629 and 1643, thousands of new colonists arrived in New England, helping provide stability for the colony and the development of the "New England Way." What was the "New England Way?"

3. Describe the houses of the typical second-generation of New Englanders.

Governing New England

When the Massachusetts Bay colony was established, only those who were members of the Massachusetts Bay Company had the right to govern the colony. Many investors intended to remain in England, having an interest in colonization only as far as it could make them a profit.

But it quickly became clear that independent-minded Puritans would not easily follow those who rested comfortably in England. In August, 1629, all stockholders of the company agreed to either migrate to America and participate directly in the colony or sell their shares of investment. This meant that, early in the history of the Massachusetts Bay colony, the colonists who migrated there had control of how the colony was to be governed.

This helped give Massachusetts a different kind of power base from other colonies. Massachusetts residents more distinctly broke from England and did not rely on outside leadership. Most of the investors in the company sold their stock. By December of 1630, fewer than 20 of the 2,000 colonists in Massachusetts had been members of the stock company.

In addition, local rule received a boost when over 100 male colonists, in October 1630, requested they be made freemen, or members of the community with full rights. The Massachusetts Bay Company granted the men this important status, but only if they were Puritans. This did not satisfy those settlers in the colony who were "strangers," who continued to clamor for their right to vote.

As long as the number of freemen was limited to only those who were Puritans, the number of voters remained small. Under the original charter, a General Court had been established, which included a governor and his deputy, a board of magistrates who advised the governor, and the members of the corporation, the freemen.

The General Court met four times annually. During the remainder of the year, the governor, his deputy (also known as a lieutenant governor) and the board of magistrates governed the colony. The freemen elected these magistrates each year. But the freemen remained dissatisfied with this system. They had no direct voice in the decision-making processes of the colony. And their political power was limited because they lived so scattered from one another.

To help remedy this problem, it became the tradition for each Puritan town and village to send two men to the General Court, called deputies. Such men could sit in on the meetings of the General Court. By 1644, an official split was recognized between the deputies and the assistants to the governor. The deputies met as a lower house of the legislature, while the governor and his assistants met as the upper house.

What had developed throughout the 1630s and early 1640s was a unique system of New World government. Changes in the corporate structure of the Massachusetts Bay Company had led to expanded voting rights for those male adults called freemen. In addition, the split between the freemen-deputies and the governor's assistants had created a two house legislature, or bicameral.

Today, the United States Congress operates as such a legislative body, as do the state legislatures of 49 of the 50 states. The only state to operate its government as one house (unicameral) is Nebraska. In these early innovations, a form of representative democracy established its roots.

Review and Write

1. Why do you think the Puritans established self-government so quickly?

2. When the Massachusetts Bay colony was originally founded, the investors who remained in England governed the colony. Why did this system not work well in New England?

3. When the freemen became dissatisfied with the system of governance, how did the problem get solved?

Dissent Among Believers

Even as the colonial government of Massachusetts provided the root of American democracy, the political system in the colony was not exactly perfect. From the beginning, the New England colonies founded by the Puritans, such as Plymouth and Massachusetts, were directly connected to the religion of the people. Political leaders had to be members of the Puritan faith. While this system gave support to Puritans, it did not appeal to those who were not themselves members of that sect.

Governor Winthrop believed that Massachusetts Bay colony had been established by God's will and that the people of the colony should be prepared and willing to follow the will of his representatives—the Puritan elders and ministers. While such leaders expected all Puritans to act, think, and believe the same, resulting in a harmony between all members of like faith, some Puritans pursued different religious ideas.

One such independent-minded Puritan was Roger Williams. A young minister who came to Massachusetts in 1631, Williams was more conservative about theology than many other Puritans. While Winthrop believed in the hope of eventually "purifying" the Church of England, Williams thought true believers should sever all ties with the English state church. By 1633, Williams was actively and publicly speaking against the king of England.

Even though Governor Winthrop was Williams's friend, he knew Williams posed a threat to the colony of Massachusetts. In October 1635, the governor's assistants summoned Williams to explain himself. Before them, the controversial minister was penitent, but once he returned home to Salem, he began speaking out against the Massachusetts Bay charter (which had been issued by the king whom Williams hated).

Williams soon announced his belief that the elected leaders of the colony did not have the right to make laws regarding one's practice of religion. Such statements prompted serious action and

Massachusetts leaders voted to banish Williams from the colony. In 1636, Williams made his way out of the colony to Narragansett Bay, where he lived with the local Indians. In time, Williams bought land from the natives and founded the town of Providence.

Another challenge to Puritan authority in Massachusetts was a woman named Anne Hutchinson. Arriving in the colony with her husband in 1634, Hutchinson became well known for her religious discussion meetings. A very devout woman, she came to criticize some Boston ministers for, according to Hutchinson, their lack of piety.

Such criticism of Puritan leaders by a woman led the General Court to call Hutchinson to make an accounting of her accusations. Standing before the Puritan men of the Court in November 1637, Hutchinson argued well against their accusations that she had stepped out of line as a Puritan woman. But when she claimed that she had received a direct revelation from God, her words sealed her fate. The General Court ordered her and her family banished from the colony. In May 1638, "Mistress Anne" and her family moved to join Roger Williams on Narragansett Bay. A few years later, Hutchinson and others established a new community at Westchester. In time, sadly, she and members of her family were killed in an Indian raid.

Review and Write

Why do you think the General Court thought dissenters such as Roger Williams and Anne Hutchinson were such a threat?

Test II

Part I.

Matching. *Match the answers shown below with the statements given above. Place the letters of the correct answers in the spaces below.*

1. The founder of New France
2. An Indian word meaning "where the river narrows"
3. French colonists who came to New France to work as farmers on someone else's land
4. Wealthy French colonists who came to New France to own land worked by others
5. French trapper type known for his hunting and trading in the forest regions of Canada
6. French trapper type known for traveling further west out onto the Canadian Plains
7. French coureur de bois who explored eastern Canada, and south to Chesapeake Bay
8. Black-robed priests who converted Indians in Canada to Christianity
9. French fur trader who accompanied French priest on 1672 voyage down Mississippi River
10. Fort established by French explorer Sieur de La Salle
11. Name of Henry Hudson's ship that sailed to America in 1609-10
12. Dutch settlement established on Hudson river in site of modern-day Albany, New York

A. seigneurs   B. Etienne Brule   C. Crèvecoeur   D. Fort Orange
E. Kebec   F. coureurs de bois   G. Jesuits   H. Louis Joliet
I. Samuel de Champlain   J. inhabitants   K. voyageurs   L. *Half-Moon*

1. ____ 2. ____ 3. ____ 4. ____ 5. ____ 6. ____ 7. ____ 8. ____ 9. ____ 10. ____ 11. ____ 12. ____

Part II.

Matching. *Match the answers shown below with the statements given above. Place the letters of the correct answers in the spaces below.*

1. A Christian sect that wished to purify the Church of England
2. The Pilgrims intended to sail to America aboard the *Mayflower* and this ship, in 1620
3. Name of baby born on the voyage on the Mayflower
4. Agreement among Separatists and "stranger" males to accept self-rule in the New World
5. Site of colony established by the Pilgrims along the Massachusetts coastline
6. Name of Native American who helped the Pilgrims; had been to England and spoke English
7. Served as the only professional soldier among the Pilgrims
8. First elected governor of the Pilgrim settlement in America; died during first winter of 1621
9. Second colony formed by Puritans in New England in 1630
10. Landing in New England of 1000 immigrants on 11 ships in 1630
11. Type of New England house featuring roof with one side steeper than the other
12. Government created under original charter for Massachusetts Bay

A. Mayflower Compact   B. Plymouth   C. Miles Standish   D. Massachusetts Bay
E. Puritans   F. Speedwell   G. "Great Migration"   H. General Court
I. Oceanus   J. Squanto   K. John Carver   L. saltbox

1. ____ 2. ____ 3. ____ 4. ____ 5. ____ 6. ____ 7. ____ 8. ____ 9. ____ 10. ____ 11. ____ 12. ____

Establishing New England Towns

The pressure to conform to the religious standards of the leaders of the Massachusetts Bay Colony, and by the arrival of more and more people led some people in New England to begin building new colonies. This movement led to the establishment of colonies in Connecticut, Rhode Island, and New Hampshire, as well as a variety of scattered settlements within the modern-day state of Massachusetts.

The pattern typically began with the founding of a settlement first. A colony required a charter from the English monarch, which sometimes took years. By the time such a land grant became official, colonists were already living in the new colony.

The colony of Rhode Island was first populated by those who, for a variety of reasons, left the Massachusetts Bay Colony. The dissident Roger Williams and the banished Anne Hutchinson were among the first. Williams helped establish the settlement at Providence. The modern-day city of Portsmouth was settled in 1638 by 18 people from the Massachusetts Bay Colony. Their leader was a close friend of Anne Hutchinson.

In 1643, Roger Williams went to England to obtain a charter from King Charles I. But while he was there, Charles faced a civil war, led by the Puritans, which ended with the king's beheading and the rise to power of the Puritans. Naturally, Williams received his land charter in 1644 from his fellow believers in Parliament.

By 1647, the towns of Providence and Portsmouth, as well as new settlements at Newport and Warwick banded together and formed a separate colony called Rhode Island. The government the colonists established was similar to that of Massachusetts, including a governor, board of assistants, and an assembly. In Rhode Island, however, non-church members were allowed to vote. Also, towns retained veto power over the laws established by the assembly. It they chose not to recognize a certain law as applying to them, they had the power to say so. This was an attractive incentive to future colonists.

Other dissatisfied residents of Massachusetts moved into the rich, fertile valley of the Connecticut River. In 1633, some Plymouth residents established a settlement they called Windsor, situated on the river, about 40 miles from Long Island Sound. Others followed. Three years later, additional colonists came from the Massachusetts Bay Colony and settled in Windsor, Wethersfield, and Hartford, all located close to one another on the Connecticut.

By 1637, these townspeople formed a government that included a governor, assistants, and nine representatives, three from each town. Their written constitution was called the Fundamental Orders and it was adopted in 1639. This document gave all men the right to vote, regardless of church membership. The new colony was named for the Connecticut River. Although Connecticut grew and new settlements were built, including coastal New Haven, the colony did not receive a charter until 1662.

Other colonists established settlements north of the Massachusetts Bay Colony. One early resident of the colony that became New Hampshire was Anne Hutchinson's brother-in-law, who established a settlement known as Exeter. Still others built the town of Hampton. Many early New Hampshire settlers were dissidents. By 1679, King Charles II granted the colony of New Hampshire a charter.

Review and Write

1. What often led New England colonists to establish new settlements and colonies?

2. As more and more people came to New England, the pressure grew to establish ne colonies. What was the typical settlement pattern that developed in New England?

3. One of the early branch-off colonies of New England was Rhode Island. What role did Roger Williams have in the establishment of this new colony of English settlers?

Puritan Towns and Schools

Land distribution in the New England colonies was, from the beginning, different from the pattern established in other colonies, such as Virginia and Maryland. While the Tidewater colonies came to rely on the headright system, which provided individuals 50 acres of land once they paid their ship passage and arrived in the New World, the New England model relied on people living in close proximity to one another and holding land communally.

The pattern in New England was designed to encourage town settlement and growth. Called the town system, it began in the Massachusetts Bay Colony and spread from there to the other colonies. In design, it could not have been more simple. A group of families banded together to establish a new town. They approached the General Court for permission.

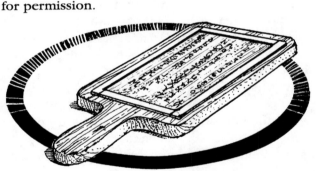

Before granting their permission, the members of the Court examined each member of the group to ensure they were all Puritans. The proposed site was also checked out, and the Court made certain the proposed location could support the group. A water source was determined, the fertility of the soil examined, and questions concerning how the site might be defended were answered.

Once the General Court was assured of all such details, they would grant the land to the would-be settlers. Town officials, known as proprietors, were then appointed. Typically, town grants were issued in plots measuring six miles square. It was up to the proprietors to divide up the property to the various families of the group. Plans were made to build a church and locate a minister. Often, a grassy meadow was chosen as the center of the town, called the village green.

The green often became the middle of the town proper. Private family dwellings, as well as a school, Puritan meetinghouse, and blacksmith shop were usually the first buildings built surrounding the village green. If a stream or river flowed nearby, the colonists built a gristmill where their corn was ground into meal.

Since most colonists were farmers, they cleared fields relatively near their new village. The fields were divided into long strips and given out to the member families. Any potential farmland not assigned to a family was controlled by the town proprietors. Some farmland was held in common by the people which was used as grazing land for their cattle, sheep, and other domesticated animals.

The town meetinghouse was not only used for Puritan worship services. It also provided a meeting site for the townsmen to assemble to discuss town business and other related issues. During such town meetings, the freemen selected those they wished to represent them at the General Court in Boston. Such meetings were still another form of early democracy in colonial America. Voting was limited to male landowners, but it provided another seed for the development of representative government.

Such towns also established schools for their children. A 1647 Massachusetts law required every Puritan town having a population of 50 families to establish a school for young students. Towns numbering 100 families were to establish a "grammar" school for older boys where they were taught Latin as a preparation for college. Such an emphasis on schooling in New England produced the highest literacy rate of any of the colonies—a rate even higher than in most of Europe.

Review and Write

How was land typically distributed to colonial residents of New England?

34

New England Indian Wars

As English colonists expanded into new corners of New England, establishing more settlements, and receiving charters for additional colonies, the Native Americans of the region began to feel the pressure of encroachment. New settlements were often located in fertile valleys or along the coast near prime fishing waters, places Indians had traditionally occupied. This led to eventual conflict between Indians and the ever-increasing numbers of English colonists.

When violence erupted, however, it was not always as simple as whites versus Indians. Some Indian tribes had early on allied with English settlers to gain new strength against another traditional Indian enemy. The result was a pattern of alliances and loyalties leading to the deaths of Indians at the hands of other Indians.

At the heart of the problems arising between the English settlers and the New England Native Americans were their different concepts concerning land. The English, as other Europeans, believed in private land ownership by individuals. Such property rights were foreign to Indians who looked at the land as something to be used by a group living communally. Native Americans never understood the concept of someone "owning" property.

This difference caused many problems when the English and members of an Indian tribe made a treaty concerning the land. When a chief "signed" a treaty, the English thought he was surrendering any right to that piece of property. Such chiefs believed they were simply agreeing to "share" the use of the land with the new white arrivals.

Armed clashes with Native Americans came quickly after the arrival of the Pilgrims. In 1623, the Wampanoag chief Massasoit convinced the Pilgrims' military leader, Miles Standish, to attack a neighboring enemy of the Wampanoags, the Massachusetts who lived north of Plymouth. When Standish did so, he returned with the head of the tribe's sachem and placed it on a pike outside the settlement's entrance. Even their allies, the Wampanoags, soon understood they would have to watch the English closely, calling them *wotowquenange*, meaning "cutthroats."

In 1636, the colonists went to war with the Pequot tribe whom they accused of killing a Boston trader. In fact, the Pequots had nothing to do with his death. The Narragansets joined the colonists in fighting the Pequots. The Pequot War resulted in a massacre at their main village, including the deaths of women and children. Many others were killed or forced to become slaves.

A generation later, another Indian war in New England erupted. By 1671, Plymouth Indian leaders forced the Wampanoags to accept English authority over their traditional lands. This humiliating decision stirred the tribe against the Puritans.

A sachem named Metacom (also known as King Philip), son of Massasoit, led his people against the English, breaking a half-century of alliance with the New Englanders. Soon, other tribes joined the Wampanoags. Bloodshed spread throughout the region.

King Philip's War lasted about one year. Metacom and his warriors burned homes and corncribs, and killed Englishmen. The settlement of Pocumtuck was set ablaze. By the summer of 1676, colonial militia forces had driven most of the Indians into hiding. When Metacom himself was killed (shot by an Indian guide working for the English), he was decapitated and his body hacked to pieces. By the time the war ended, about 50 percent of the Indians living in New England had been either killed or had fled the region.

Review and Write

Why were colonial Indian wars often not simply struggles between whites and Indians?

Bacon's Rebellion

In the same year New England exploded into a full-blown Indian war, so Indian-related violence erupted in Maryland and Virginia. Beginning in January of 1676, Indian raids in Virginia caused the deaths of dozens of colonists. Backwoods settlers feared for their lives, and many fled to the east, seeking sanctuary from Indian attack.

As they arrived in the established towns of Tidewater planters and the more wealthy families of Virginia, a call went out from both Virginia planters and frontier families demanding protection from the colonial governor, Sir William Berkeley. But Berkeley was cautious about raising military parties to raid against alleged Indian aggressors. Such an encounter could easily expand into a full-scale Indian war.

When Berkeley seemed hesitant to come to the rescue of frontier men and women fearful of Indian attack, they turned on their governor. In part, the animosity between Berkeley and the frontier families was nothing new. The Virginia of 1676 was extremely different from the Virginia of 1607 Jamestown. Society had developed, separating colonists into two groups. One group was older families who owned large plantations and great wealth. The second was the yeoman farmers of the frontier.

The frontiersmen were second and even third generation arrivals to Virginia. Many had come to the Tidewater as indentured servants with no legal access to land. The old headright system that distributed 50 acres to each new arrival to Virginia had not been available to them when they arrived, for indentured servants generally could not pay their own passage. As a result, a common pattern had developed throughout the century. When indentured servants completed their indenture, they received their "freedom dues," of clothing, seed, and tools, but they still did not own land. Many of them moved up the various Virginia rivers and took up residence on land that was not theirs legally. Such people were called "squatters" and the Virginia aristocracy considered them commoners.

A cycle of poverty had developed for the frontier squatters by the 1670s. Such people looked jealously at men such as Governor Berkeley as the holders of wealth and power. But one such man, a recent arrival to Virginia named Nathaniel Bacon, a well-bred Englishman who had already been invited to serve on Berkeley's council, sided with the frontiersmen against Berkeley. In the spring of 1676, Bacon led a group of planters and their servants in his own campaign against the Indians. When Bacon returned to Jamestown after the raid, an angry Berkeley had him arrested.

When the frontiersmen appeared to rally behind the imprisoned Bacon, Berkeley agreed to release him, but only after Bacon agreed to halt his actions. But by June, Bacon returned to Jamestown with 500 followers demanding permission from the governor to kill Indians once again. Berkeley agreed, only to change his mind later and call for Bacon's arrest once again. Bacon then turned on the governor, marched his men into Jamestown, drove Berkeley out, and burned the town.

Bacon's Rebellion was short-lived, however, for Bacon died the next month of dysentery. He had called for a revolt against Berkeley and talked of independence from English control in Virginia. Bacon was the wrong person to lead a real political revolution, for he killed Indians savagely and without provocation. But, his challenge to royal authority in Virginia brought armed conflict between colonial commoners and British power a century before the American Revolution of the 1770s.

Review and Write

1. Do you think Bacon was a hero or not? Explain your answer.

2. The frontiersmen who faced Indian attack along the Virginia frontier were typically poor squatters who did not own their own land. What circumstances in the colonies had led to the development of such a class of poor individual?

The Puritans and Their Religion

Because their religion was so important to them as a daily reminder of how to lead honest, sober lives, while remaining keenly aware of God's will for everyone, the Puritans are often remembered for little else today. The word "puritanical" is often used as a negative reference for someone who is prudish, narrow-minded, overly-strict when disciplining, and self-righteous.

However, the Puritans should not be thought of so simply. They were not ignorant people opposed to everything fun. Enjoying the company they shared with their fellow believers could bring them joy.

Unlike the stereotype, Puritans did not always wear drab, black and white clothing. They enjoyed color, and their clothes often featured deep shades of orange, red, blue, yellow, purple, and brown, hues they called the "sadd colors." But they were opposed to wearing flashy, gaudy, or elaborate clothing that made someone stand out as if he or she wanted to be noticed.

Their religion, however, sometimes caused the Puritans to become overly pious and judgmental. They believed their ideas about religion were true and that differing ideas might constitute false teaching. Puritans thought that strict morality played an important role in helping keep Christians pure and unspotted from the world around them. As a result, the Puritans created many rules about how to act on a day-to-day basis. Their concept of good and evil recognized the Devil, Satan, as a destroyer, one who could gain a foothold in the heart of any Puritan who made wrong moral choices.

The Puritans took the power of Satan so seriously they believed he could possess people. Sometimes, in fact, evil-minded people might willingly become loyal to the Devil and do his will regularly. Such people were often thought to be witches.

Without question, the Puritans believed in the reality of witchcraft. But, then, so did nearly everyone else in the world. It was not unique to them or their religion. In fact, the belief in witches in Europe led to the deaths of thousands of individuals, most of them women. During one three-month period in Switzerland alone, in 1515, more than 500 witches were burned at the stake.

The Puritan belief in witches was a basic religious concept that helped explain some important theological issues to their satisfaction. Their reasoning followed this line of logic: Through God, good exists in the world. Evil exists through the works of Satan. While God would never cause bad things to happen to good people, Satan would be more than happy to oblige. His followers on earth sometimes help him.

The Puritan belief in witches, then, explained events that had no other explanation. When a "natural" catastrophe struck, such as a flood or a poor crop harvest, or when a minister died of a disease, it must have been the work of witches.

When, for example, in 1651, a Connecticut militiaman named Henry Stiles was shot "accidentally" by fellow recruit Thomas Allen, after Allen swung his musket around and hit a tree, a fiery-tempered woman in the community, Lydia Gilbert, was accused of being a witch and "caus-ing" Stiles's death. Since Gilbert did not perform her regular Christian duties and was known to have a grievance against Stiles, the accusation and Gilbert's conviction made, to the Puritan mind, perfect sense. Gilbert was branded for her devilish crime. The Puritan belief in witchcraft provided answers for events that occurred that would otherwise have remained a mystery.

Witchcraft in Salem

Since the Puritans of New England believed that everything that happened in their world happened for a reason, their belief in witchcraft helped explain why events in the lives of people occurred as they did. It was God's will that witchcraft existed, therefore, when a boat overturned at sea during a violent storm or the family cow died or a hunter returned with no kill or a keg of ale soured in its barrel, the Puritans examined the circumstances and could find the cause of such calamities in witchcraft.

Actually, compared to witch-hunts in Europe where thousands were tried and executed during the same centuries, colonial witchcraft cases were not that common. Between 1630 and 1700, the number of New England trials involving people accused of being either witches or warlocks (male witches) numbered around 100. Of that number, approximately 40 resulted in the death of the accused, usually by hanging. (There were no incidents of witch burnings in the British colonies at any time.)

One of the most famous witchcraft events in the history of colonial America took place in the 1690s in a small New England settlement called Salem. It was a tragic, yet natural extension of the Puritan beliefs on the subject. The sad series of events began when a group of Puritan girls began to take seriously some stories about witchcraft as told by a West Indian servant-woman named Tituba. These scary stories, which included tales about the Devil, probably frightened the girls who became psychologically fixated on their stories.

When Tituba taught the girls, including a nine-year-old named Elizabeth Parris and an 11-year-old named Abigail Williams, to bark like dogs and to pretend to experience a violent shaking as if they were possessed by an unseen being, their world of pretend play and real fear took a dark turn.

During a church service, the girls began to speak out, pretending to see yellow birds on the minister's head, and other apparitions which no one else could see. Although the girls were pretending, their statements were taken seriously by adults who believed in witchcraft. When the girls accused some women of the community—not only Tituba, but a pair of women named Sarah Good and Sarah Osburn—of bewitching them, the community of Salem was soon intent on discovering the witchcraft in their village and putting a stop to it.

Whether the girls came to believe in their stories or realized they had taken events too far and could not possibly confess they had made it all up, is not certain.

But they continued to accuse others, and demonstrated their possessions even more madly, by throwing screaming fits and claiming to see things others could not.

As fear gripped the community of Salem, even adults accused other adults of being witches. Witch Examiner Court proceedings were held and the girls were allowed to testify against several innocent people. The girls claimed to feel blows against their bodies and pinches caused by unseen hands. Several of those accused were found guilty. Over 100 citizens of Salem were accused of practicing Satan's black arts, and 20 were convicted and sentenced to death. (Two of the town's dogs were also found guilty.) All but one were women and all were hanged. The single male killed was crushed to death.

Years later, when the girls were older, some of them confessed that the fear and death they caused in Salem in 1692 had been based on lies—stories told by adults they wanted to believe and so, took seriously.

Review and Write

1. Why do you think the people of Salem believed the young girls who claimed to know who in their community were witches?

2. Give the statistics regarding the number of people who were accused of witchcraft in colonial America.

Founding the Carolinas

In time, Massachusetts and Virginia, two of the first English colonies established in the New World, became the most populous of all the colonies in North America. Throughout the 1600s, and even into the early 1700s, other colonies were also founded, including some already mentioned: Plymouth, Maryland, Connecticut, Rhode Island, and New Hampshire. Before 1735, 13 separate English colonies had been established along the Atlantic seaboard of North America, stretching from New England south to Georgia, the last of the 13 to be established.

Some colonies did not remain independent of others. The first New England colony of Plymouth, founded by the Pilgrims, was later absorbed into Massachusetts in 1691. Massachusetts also controlled territory to the north which today is the state of Maine.

Several colonies were established during a single generation beginning after the rise of Charles II to the throne of England. His father, Charles I, had been beheaded during the English Civil War of the 1640s, and a Puritan government ran England for 11 years until 1660, the year Charles II became king. This "restoring" of the English monarchy brought on the establishment of the "Restoration Colonies."

The first of these colonies came about in 1663 when Charles II issued the first of his colonial charters. This colony, called Carolina (the Latin form of *Charles* is "Carolus"), was located south of Virginia stretching down to Spanish Florida. Immigrants from Virginia had already begun occupying land in the region. By 1664, eight men—nobles who were friends of the king—controlled the colony.

While earlier economic conditions in England had helped encourage colonization of the New World, many of those circumstances had changed significantly by the late 17th century, making it difficult for the Carolina proprietors to attract enough colonists to their New World venture.

One of the early proprietors, an English aristocrat named Sir Anthony Ashley Cooper did develop a new idea of governing the colony, hoping to lure colonists. With the aid and direction of his secretary, the highly intellectual political philosopher John Locke, Cooper introduced the "Fundamental Constitutions for Carolina," in 1669.

The document described plans for a highly complex social system with men, called "landgraves" and "caciques," holding large tracts of land, allowing them to establish a system of English nobility in the New World. Yet such men were to share local governing with the smaller, less affluent landholders.

In addition, proprietors such as Cooper offered generous land grants, with headrights of up to 150 acres per person. Such colonists were also promised significant political and civil rights, such as the freedom of representative assembly, religious toleration, and the right to hold slaves.

However, the colony did not develop quickly. As late as 1675, only 5000 people lived in the northern half of Carolina. This "North Carolina" was home to both large tobacco plantations and small farms.

Another pocket of settlement in Carolina centered in the southern portion of the colony, around a coastal port called Charles Town, or modern-day Charleston. Many of the settlers who occupied "South Carolina" came from an English colony in the Caribbean called Barbados. This island had become crowded with Englishmen by the 1670s, as well as Africans who were worked as slaves.

Hundreds of both Englishmen and slaves relocated to Carolina. Others arrived from other places. After 1685, several hundred French Huguenots (Protestants) sailed to the New World to live in "South Carolina." By 1700, South Carolina's non-Indian population stood at 6000, of whom nearly half were black slaves.

Before 1691, the northern and southern Carolinas were administered as two separate colonies, each having its own government. For a short period, an attempt was made to unite the two halves under one governor, but traditional patterns of settlement won out. In 1712, the Carolinas were officially separated into two, distinct colonies.

New Netherland Falls to the English

While King Charles II helped establish the Carolinas as proprietorship colonies along the southern seaboard of North America, he also set his sights on establishing another Restoration colony to the north, where, by the 1660s, the Dutch colony of New Netherland had become a successful and lucrative colonial venture.

From the colony's establishment in the 1620s, New Netherland had cornered the fur trade with the Iroquois, a powerful union of tribes in modern-day New York. Both the Iroquois and the Dutch had pushed out competition from the region. The Iroquois, through a series of conflicts called the Beaver Wars, had forced the Hurons from the region during the 1640s, a tribe that had controlled the fur trade for many years.

The Dutch, with equal aggression, had forced their European neighbors, the Swedes, from their trading posts along the Delaware River in 1655. The Swedes had established New Sweden in 1638, located in modern-day Delaware.

Dutch ships attacked the Swedish settlement of Fort Christina (named in honor of the queen of Sweden)—the site of Wilmington, Delaware today—and successfully took over the colony without a shot being fired. While many Swedes remained in North America, they chose to live under Dutch control. (Incidentally, the primary contribution made by the Swedes to American frontier history was the introduction of the log cabin, a building type popular in Sweden during that period.)

But now, it was England's turn to intimidate the Dutch in New Netherland. In 1664, the English sent four ships to capture the Dutch colony. When the ships arrived, the Dutch governor, a fiery leader named Peter Stuyvesant, refused to surrender his colony under threat from English guns.

Stuyvesant had come to the Dutch colony as a young man in his late teens. He was feisty, with a quick temper. As director general, he ruled New Amsterdam with an iron fist. (In fact, Stuyvesant had a wooden leg held together with silver nails. Often he would bang his leg against a table during council meetings to intimidate opponents.)

Now, with the English at the Dutch door, Stuyvesant was prepared to make a stand to defend his colony from attack. But his subjects would not follow him. Stuyvesant was not a popular ruler with the people of New Amsterdam. Some had reported him earlier to Dutch officials in Holland. When the director general became aware of such criticism, he had threatened to kill any who opposed him: "If anyone tries to report to the Netherlands again, I will make him a foot shorter. Then I will send the pieces to Holland and let him seek help in that way."

Not only would his people not support him now, the Dutch had little gunpowder and few lead bullets on hand with which to defend themselves. Just as the Swedes had been forced to surrender to the Dutch without firing a shot, so now the Dutch surrendered to the English warships in their harbor at New Amsterdam on September 8, 1664.

Now the territory was English land. The name of the colony was changed to New York after one of the men chosen by Charles II to serve as proprietor of the colony, the Duke of York.

Review and Write

How had the Dutch taken control of the fur trade in the region of New Netherland?

Establishing New Jersey

James, the Duke of York, brother to King Charles II, received the land grant for the newly acquired colony of New York after English warships sailed into Manhattan harbor, forcing the surrender of New Amsterdam. While the residents of the trade community found themselves, in 1664, under English control, little in the colony immediately changed. Those living in the colony, for the most part, remained even after Dutch rule had ended.

The people of the collective settlements of New Netherland were a mixed group of colonists. Among New Amsterdam's population, 18 languages were spoken. Second only to Boston in size, New Amsterdam (originally Manhattan) was home to Dutch, Swedes, Finns, English, and others, including dozens of Jews from Brazil. In the mid-1650s, New Netherland was the only Atlantic seaboard colony to allow Jews to settle there. There were also many blacks living in New Amsterdam—about one out of every five residents.

Under English control, the various peoples living in the former Dutch colony were granted the status of English subjects by 1674. Less than a decade later, the Duke of York allowed the colonists to establish a representative assembly. When the Duke of York's grant was created, it included the lands of modern-day New Jersey, for this region had been part of New Netherland. Even before the end of 1664, the duke ceded the land to a pair of his friends, Sir George Carteret and Lord John Berkeley. Carteret and Berkeley were two of the original eight proprietors of the Carolina colony.

Almost immediately, the two New Jersey proprietors gave out land to interested settlers. In February 1665, to attract immigrants, Carteret and Berkeley announced the Concessions and Agreements Act. This document promised the establishment of a general assembly, the right to free and open trade for all residents, and religious toleration to any Protestant sect (Catholics were excluded.) The proprietors appointed a lieutenant governor and a council of advisors. The general assembly was granted the power to tax the

residents of New Jersey.

As for land concessions, the proprietors retained ownership of one out of every seven acres. Immigrants to New Jersey were promised 150 acres for every family head, as well as an additional 150 acres for each servant. Any servant who remained in the colony for four years received his own land grant of 75 acres.

In 1665, a cousin of Sir George Carteret, Philip, sailed to the colony to become its first lieutenant governor. His first problem as leader was to unravel the tangled web of conflicting land claims. Some settlers' claims predated the transfer of the colony from the Duke of York to Carteret and Berkeley. Some residents never even accepted the authority of Philip Carteret to govern them. By 1674, Berkeley sold his interest in the colony to a pair of men belonging to a religious sect known as the Quakers. One of these men then sold his share to a group of Quakers. One of their members was William Penn, later the founder of the colony of Pennsylvania.

In an effort to reorganize the colony, Carteret divided New Jersey in half, granting the Quakers West Jersey, while he kept East Jersey for himself. In time, the Quakers dominated the region on both sides of the Delaware River, a development that occurred at the hands of William Penn.

William Penn's Colony

William Penn, the founder of the English colony called Pennsylvania, did not begin his colonization efforts there, but rather, in helping organize portions of the New Jersey colony for Quaker immigrants.

Penn was unlike many of those other proprietors who founded colonies granted to them by various English monarchs. Their colonial efforts were often motivated by selfish ambition or greed, and their colonies often suffered under corruption carried out in the name of the proprietors.

At all times, as he worked hard at colonizing in America, Penn remained a fair-minded man, one known for his personal integrity and honesty. He organized colonies to give aid and sanctuary to his fellow Quakers. He thought it important to establish colonies with the public in mind.

As a young man, William Penn lived the life of a rich, upper-class gentleman. His father, Sir William Penn, served as the lord admiral of England for Charles II. Penn was highly educated, attending both Oxford and Cambridge. He entered the royal diplomatic corps. But, in his early twenties, Penn converted to a Protestant religious group called the Society of Friends, often referred to as the Quakers. The Friends believed in a simple Christianity, thought of all people as equals, refused to go to war, and would not pay to support either their king or the Church of England. They, including Penn, were regularly jailed for such beliefs.

More than a decade after Penn's conversion, his father died. King Charles II had borrowed heavily from the elder Penn and, in 1681, he offered to repay the debt to William. However, already involved in the Quaker colony in New Jersey, William Penn requested the debt to be paid in American land. The king was more than ready to do so. He granted a charter to Penn for a colony that extended from the Delaware River 5 degrees longitude west and from the 40th degree to the 43rd degree of north latitude. While the king had no idea how much property this included, it was, in fact, larger than all of England. And the next year,

it was enlarged still further when Penn convinced the Duke of York to grant him additional land west of Delaware Bay.

Charles II named the land grant Pennsylvania, which meant "Penn's Woods." Penn, as a true Quaker, felt the name was ostentatious. Colonies were named after royalty—Virginia, Carolina, Maryland, New York—but the king insisted, explaining: "It is not you but your father I honor."

Penn instantly announced the opening of his colony to his fellow Quakers as a New World sanctuary. He intended his colony to be as idealistic as possible. Penn sent a cousin, William Markham, to Pennsylvania, to announce to anyone living there that the land was now part of Penn's colony. Markham selected the site for the colony's capital, Philadelphia, meaning "brotherly love."

Penn laid out the plan of government for his colony, calling it the Frame of Government. As proprietor, he was to be governor. In addition, there was to be a deputy governor and a council of assistants, elected by the colony's freeholders, who were themselves landowners. In 1682, that assembly voted to pass the Great Law, which gave religious freedom to all Christians. To ensure friendly relations with local Indians, Penn "purchased" the land from them and closely monitored all trade between Indians and non-Indians.

Pennsylvania became a popular colony and in its first ten years, Philadelphia grew to a population of 4000. But Penn's dream of creating a colony based on "brotherly love" did not actually come true.

Review and Write

1. How did William Penn's conversion to the Society of Friends change his life?

2. As Penn established his colony of Pennsylvania, he pursued policies that made his colony a model for others. What did Penn do in establishing Pennsylvania that made it an example to other future colonies?

Troubles for William Penn

Just as William Penn was different from many other colonial proprietors, so his colony was also different. The same was true of his city, Philadelphia.

It was one of the few early colonial cities in America to qualify as a "planned community." Penn established his city as a series of interconnected rectangles. The streets were laid out in a checkerboard pattern. He included open, public squares and green spaces, not intended as public grazing pastures but as firebreaks. In 1666, London had experienced a violent and destructive fire that had destroyed much of the city. Penn was probably thinking of this tragedy when he organized Philadelphia.

Even as the streets were laid out, he ordered that the most noble and handsome-looking trees be retained to help make the city more beautiful. Some of the first streets of Philadelphia were named for various trees that dotted the landscape, such as "Chestnut," "Pine," and "Walnut." Penn then wrote advertising pamphlets to encourage immigrants to come live in his new town. To attract would-be merchants and shopkeepers, Penn wrote: "*Your city-lot is a whole street ... that by God's blessing ... will naturally grow in ... reputation and profit. I am sure I have not turned my back upon any offer that tended to its prosperity.*"

Such efforts by Penn succeeded. Merchants were immediately attracted to Pennsylvania, and they soon dominated the city of Philadelphia. Between 1682 and 1689, over 50 merchants and traders established businesses in the young city. Thirty more were in business by 1700.

But, for all his plans to make his colony a success, Penn was not personally successful. He had a lifelong problem with money. After inheriting his father's fortune, he quickly spent it, paying little attention to his expenses. This fact, his personal money problems, provided an additional incentive behind his colonizing efforts.

Penn first ran into trouble with his colony when he reduced the number of council members from 72 to 18. His motive was to make governing the colony more efficient. But Penn proved to be an unpopular colonial administrator. He insisted in overseeing the smallest detail concerning the day-to-day decisions made as proprietor. Such micro-management, plus a perception on the part of some of his colonists that he was stuffing the assembly with his own supporters, gave Penn more grief than happiness. After two years in Pennsylvania, Penn left for England in 1684. He did not return to Pennsylvania for another 15 years.

When he returned in 1699 to recover control of his colony, he failed. The assembly was insistent on running Pennsylvania, and Penn found himself caught up in a political power struggle. Then, in 1701, he received word that the English monarchy intended to take control of all proprietary colonies. Penn left for England to defend his rights over Pennsylvania. He never returned to America again, and died in 1718.

Despite his personal failures, Penn's colony did prosper. It also became a haven for people from many countries including England, Sweden, Finland, and Holland. Scots-Irish and Germans also came to Pennsylvania by the thousands.

Review and Write

1. What did Penn do to make his colony a model for others? What problems did he face as proprietor?

2. As Penn laid out his settlement center, Philadelphia, he intended his community to be a "planned community." What did Penn do to ensure such a legacy for Philadelphia?

3. Once Penn's colony was developed, many would-be colonists were attracted to it. How did the colony develop in terms of business and commerce?

4. Although Penn intended his colony to follow an ideal pattern, he faced problems as proprietor. What were some of these problems?

—The Swedes, The Dutch, and Delaware—

One of the thirteen English colonies which had a difficult beginning was Delaware. This small colony was originally part of two different colonies before becoming separate in its own right.

Delaware, long before the arrival of the first European was home to an Indian tribe that called themselves the Leni-Lenape. They lived in small villages where they farmed, fished, and hunted. Following European contact, the Leni-Lenape began to suffer from exposure to European diseases. By 1700, many of those who survived left their homes and ultimately took up residence in Canada.

The first European power to attempt control over the region that became Delaware were the Dutch. In 1632, the Leni-Lenape granted permission to the Dutch to harpoon whales off the Delaware coast. Six years later, the Swedes arrived and built a trading post along the Delaware River which they named for their queen, Fort Christina. The Swedes were led by a former Dutch governor of New Netherland, Peter Minuit. The trade settlement soon prospered, by trading with the Indians for furs.

The Swedes introduced the log cabin to America while living in Delaware. They also brought their religion, Lutheranism, and were some of the first Europeans to raise barley and rye. They used barley to make beer, building a colonial brewery. Despite the colony's success, however, even after ten years, the Swedish settlement in Delaware was home to fewer than 200 persons.

Because of their small numbers, the Swedes were eventually harassed by the Dutch of New Netherland. The Dutch took over New Sweden by force in 1655. But Dutch dominance was short-lived; in 1664, the English took control of New Netherland from the Dutch.

Throughout these years of changeover, few colonists came to Delaware. By 1682, the under-populated Delaware became part of William Penn's land grant. Since Penn did not closely administer Delaware, the people living there organized their own assembly. By the 1690s, the settlers in Delaware began to petition Penn for recognition as a colony separate from Pennsylvania. Penn finally agreed in 1701, and by 1704, Delaware became a distinct colony, even though Penn remained the technical proprietor.

In time, most of Delaware's residents turned to tobacco growing as the source of their livelihood. Marylanders came north to establish farms, bringing their slaves with them. Towns developed, with Wilmington, built on the site of Fort Christina, serving as the chief market city, attracting Quaker merchants.

Review and Write

What kept colonists from moving to Delaware in larger numbers during the 1600s?

Oglethorpe's Dream of Georgia

While most of the original 13 British colonies in North America were founded during the 1600s, beginning with Jamestown and the Virginia colony in 1607, the last colony was established in the 1700s. And while each colony began somewhat differently from the next, the Georgia colony began in a way much different from the others.

Georgia was to be the most southern of all the thirteen colonies. It was established along the Atlantic coast in a fertile region lying between the Savannah and Altamaha Rivers. Originally, the land was granted to Sir Robert Montgomery in 1717, where he intended to govern as a military ruler, or margrave, over a colony he wanted to call the Margravate of Azilia. But his efforts proved a dismal failure.

Under his original charter, Montgomery lost his colony when he failed to settle the land and "Azilia" became part of the Carolina colony, as it had been originally. But in 1729, Carolina split north and south and the two colonies became royal domains of the king of England. Once again the future of Azilia seemed to be in question.

An Englishman named James Edward Oglethorpe became interested in Azilia almost immediately. Oglethorpe was a gentleman, educated at Oxford, and a member of Parliament. Oglethorpe was a social reformer and became interested in the subject of debtors' prison.

In 18th century England, those who could not repay their debts were placed in prison and remained there until their affairs were settled, sometimes by a charitable friend or other third party. Oglethorpe understood the ironic nature of jailing a debtor, and came to believe that such a system preyed on the poor. He thought a better answer must be made available.

In a stroke of genius, Oglethorpe suggested to King George II that the land of Azilia be opened to England's debtors as an opportunity for receiving a second chance. Colonists had been reluctant to settle in the region south of Carolina because of its close proximity to Spanish Florida. Settlements could be easily attacked by the Spanish.

What Oglethorpe suggested was the development of a colony that might serve as a bumper colony, one inhabited by common people who needed a new start in the New World, and who could provide protection from the Spanish located just to the south. In this way, the new colony was to be a military settlement.

Parliament chartered the new colony in 1732 and appointed Oglethorpe as its first governor. He sailed with 120 recruits to Charleston, South Carolina, during the 1733 winter and began immediately searching for a fertile spot which could be easily defended from Spanish invasion. He selected a site on the hills above the Savannah River, where he paced off squares of land for house lots and parks, much as Penn did in establishing Philadelphia. Oglethorpe renamed the colony Georgia, after the king, and the settlement, Savannah.

As Oglethorpe recruited colonists for his New World venture, he stipulated conditions on life in Georgia: no rum, no slaves, and the local Indians must be treated fairly. Georgia grew fairly quickly, with arrivals of many kinds of people: German Lutherans, Jews from Austria and Portugal, Scottish highlanders, and others. In ten years, 1000 settlers came to live in Georgia.

By 1753, Georgia became a royal colony. Restrictions against rum and slaves were lifted and new colonists did not treat local Indians fairly. Oglethorpe's dream was only partially successful.

Origins of New World Slavery

Centuries before contact between the Old World and the New World, slavery was commonplace in Europe. While slavery is today commonly associated with black Africans, during the century Columbus sailed to America, Italian merchants bought and sold the Slavic peoples from Eastern Europe as slaves. The word *slave* is taken from the word "Slav."

But 15th century Europeans were also trafficking in slaves who were Muslims or Africans, or sometimes both. This was especially so after a 15th-century pope excommunicated merchants who sold Christian Slavs as slaves. According to the record, the first black African slaves to be imported into Europe arrived in the Portuguese capital of Lisbon in 1441. By the mid-1400s, the black slave trade between Africa and Europe was commonplace.

Many of the early slaves brought by the Portuguese to Europe were used to raise sugar on plantations located on the northern African island of Madeira. For hundreds of years, slaves and sugar growing were commonly linked.

It comes as no surprise, then, that, following the landing of Columbus in the Caribbean in the 1490s, with the introduction of sugar to the New World, where it thrived well, that black slaves were imported to the Americas as early as 1518. By the end of the century, 25,000 African slaves were being worked to death on sugar plantations on the islands of Cuba and Hispaniola, and in South American Brazil.

The Spanish and the Portuguese imported thousands of black slaves to provide cheap labor. The work required of slaves laboring on sugar plantations and in sugar mills was so strenuous, that most slaves died within four or five years after their arrival in the New World. But the profits from sugar were so high, that the plantation owners could afford to regularly replace their overworked slaves with new ones.

Other European powers also became involved in the profiteering from slave labor in the New World. By 1630, the commercial power of the Dutch allowed them to take control of Brazil for about a generation where they imported slaves and profited from sugar production. Other New World crops, such as coffee, tobacco, and tea, needed a work force as well. Slaves worked to raise and harvest them all.

The French established sugar mills in the Caribbean, with the bulk of their investments in a sugar colony known as St. Domingue, or modern-day Haiti. Not wanting to be left out, the British seized control of the Caribbean island of Jamaica in 1655.

With lucrative markets throughout the Caribbean and Brazil, New World slavery came to involve millions of African slaves. Today, historians estimate that, between 1500 and 1850, 10 million African slaves were imported to the Western Hemisphere. The peak period of importation stretched from 1701 to 1810, years during which three out of every four slaves were shipped to the Americas, including the British colonies along the Atlantic seaboard.

Of the total number of slaves imported to the New World over nearly four centuries, approximately 50 percent were sold to work on Dutch, British, and French sugar plantations. About one-third landed in Portuguese Brazil. Spain imported 10 percent to its colonies. The smallest number, about 5 percent arrived in the British colonies of North America.

Review and Write

1. Why were nearly half of the slaves brought to the New World used on sugar plantations?

2. Prior to the arrival of Europeans in the New World, slavery was common in Europe. Where did most of the slaves in Europe come from prior to 1500?

3. Once the Spanish and Portuguese began bringing slaves to the New World from Africa, how did they treat them?

Africans Before Slavery

Nearly every western European nation participated in the African slave trade to the New World at one time of another. While the Portuguese controlled the trade through its first century, the Dutch challenged their markets and became the most prolific slave trading country of the 1600s. (The first black workers brought to the English colony of Jamestown in 1611 were imported on Dutch ships.)

English traders played a significant role in the slave trade, as well, during the 1500s. The English ship captain, John Hawkins, was among the first to carry a cargo of slaves. In London, Parliament chartered the Royal African Company, which held a monopoly in black slaving for a generation between 1672 and 1698. After the latter year, the trade was opened to any and all.

The available statistics tell the story of how important the slave trade was to English shippers during the 1700s. Throughout the 1600s, English shippers rarely ever delivered more than 10,000 slaves during any one decade. But after the turn of the century, and especially after 1730, the numbers increased dramatically. From 1731 to 1740, over 40,000 slaves were shipped across the Atlantic. During the 1740s, the number rose to nearly 60,000. By the 1760s, the tally had risen to 70,000.

Who were these victims of economic greed and of man's failure of conscience? Typically, they were natives from West Africa, living in the modern-day nations of Cape Verde south to Angola. They were members of many tribes, perhaps numbering 100 in all: Mandingos, Ashantis, Yorubas, Ibos, Sekes, Mbundus, and Bakongos.

They lived in social units centered around families who formed kinship groups. Their leaders were tribal village chiefs and clan leaders. The men of these villages often practice polygyny, the custom of taking more than one wife. Yet many of their women were not bound to the home. In fact, West African women during these centuries of the slave trade typically bore fewer children than European women. African women were also given social and economic freedom to interact in village life and even profit as merchants and traders.

They were an agricultural people, having developed elaborate and sophisticated systems of production. West African farmers raised rice, fruits, sorghum, and millet, as well as a variety of roots and vegetables. Their skills included some limited iron working. These industrious Africans cleared their farming lands by burning off the underbrush and used digging sticks, not plows, to plant and weed their crops.

By the 1500s, West African cultures included towns and trade centers where markets and shops displayed wares for sale, including human beings. Africans enslaved one another for centuries prior to the arrival of Europeans. West African slavery was a different form than was practiced in other places, however. African slavery was only temporary, rarely for a lifetime, and its victims were often captives of wars or raiding parties or those being punished for a crime they committed. Often such slaves married and any offspring were born free.

When Europeans arrived along the West African coast in the late 1400s, they found a world already deeply involved in international trade. Situated on the banks of the upper Niger River was Timbuktu which traded with Muslim caravans from the East. Slaves were a part of that trade. In no time, the African slave trade became part of the European system of trans-Atlantic shipping.

Review and Write

1. While many European nations participated in the African slave trade during the 1500s and 1600s, what examples are specifically given from your reading on this page?

2. The English became deeply involved in the slave trade business during the 1700s, as well. Provide examples through statistics provided here concerning the level of English involvement in such trade.

Slave Trading

Typically, as European nations scrambled during the 1500s and 1600s for their part of the lucrative slave trade between West Africa and the New World, they competed against one another for the coveted asiento, royal permission from the king of Spain to import slaves into the Spanish colonies and elsewhere in the Americas.

Throughout the 1500s, many of the slaves—approximately 40 percent—imported from Africa were picked up in Senegambia and Guinea. During later years, other West African regions were tapped such as the "gold coast" (modern-day Ghana), and the "slave coast" (modern-day Benin, the Ivory Coast, and Nigeria). Slave traders delivered human exports from the Congo River basin, as well. By 1650, three out of every four slaves were delivered to the coast from Angola and the Congo.

By the early 1700s, Europeans could choose from more than two dozen slave trading posts and forts which were lined up along more than 200 miles of the Gold Coast alone. These outposts were cosmopolitan swap shops of human flesh to be traded for common commodities. For example, New England traders brought distilled rum, a thick, overly-sweet alcoholic beverage, and barrels of salted cod to Africa to trade for slaves.

Many of the early New Englanders hailed from Massachusetts, but by 1750, most came from Rhode Island. A common saying among Yankee traders was: "Water your rum as much as possible and sell as much by the short measure as you can."

European buyers lined up to view the human wares, those captured on kidnapping raids, called *panyarings*, into the African interior. Slaves were held in dark prison cells or in vast open pits called *barracoons*.

The prospective purchase, often naked, was examined by merchants and ships' captains. Once a selection was made, the slave was branded on either the back or the buttocks with the merchant's mark.

How did the Europeans, many of whom practiced Christianity, justify the deportation of millions of black slaves from their traditional homelands to lives of back-breaking labor in the Americas? European traders and merchants argued that African slaves were better suited for work in the Caribbean than white workers or those of others races. They believed that Africans were able to withstand the heat and humidity of working in the tropics, since such conditions were part of their African experience.

While such a justification is based in racism, there was some truth to the argument. European laborers in the Caribbean died at a rate 10 times higher than people their same age living in Europe. But the work of the slaves shortened their lives as well. Africans died at rates twice as high as those of their same age who remained in Africa.

To ease the consciences of the European buyers in the Caribbean, slave importers often labeled their slaves as "captured in just war." While this ploy was a common ruse, most slave buyers in the Americas were careful not to ask about the details of such claims. In fact, most did not care whether it was true or not.

Review and Write

How were merchants and shippers from New England involved in the slave trade?

Horrors of the "Middle Passage"

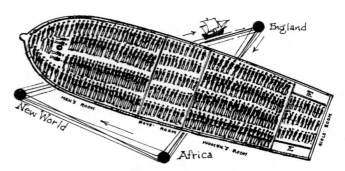

Once an unfortunate African was captured, brought in chains to the coast, and poked and prodded until he or she was bought, the next step in the brutally dehumanizing process was a sea voyage across the Atlantic to the New World. The slaves, many of them speaking languages different from one another, were completely removed from any recognizable surroundings. Many had never even seen a sailing ship and they certainly had never been onboard one. They did not understand what lay ahead for them. Torn from family, village, and familiar settings, many of these frightened slaves believed they were being delivered to a place where they would be killed and eaten.

The voyage across the Atlantic came to be called the "Middle Passage." It was the middle leg of a variety of trade "triangles" that often included a voyage from England to Africa; Africa to the New World; the New World back to England.

Slave ships were dreadful vessels designed to transport as much human cargo as possible to increase the profits of each voyage. There was no intent to create any comfort for the slaves themselves. As a result, the levels below the upper deck measured six feet in length and less than three feet high. Slaves had to lie down in cramped quarters, packed together, as one slaver said,"like herring in a barrel." Slavers jammed the slaves together, allowing no more than 18 inches of space (lying down) for each captive.

Some slavers believed that overcrowding on slave ships was not the best means of delivering slaves. They thought that additional space for each slave resulted in a greater rate of survival, giving profits a boost. But most slave ship captains forced their slaves to live with a minimum of space. Often a ship loaded more slaves than it was designed to hold. One ship, built to carry 450 slaves was more typically packed with 600 people below decks.

Below, where the slaves suffered, was a hellish world of stench, filth, heat, and human anguish. There was no consideration for sanitation, causing the hold of the vessel to reek with a sickening odor. The slaves were chained together in long rows, with the irons attached to their ankles. They generally had to lie down on hard wooden planks since there was not enough room to stand up completely.

Daily life was monotonous and depressing. Each morning the ship's crew opened up the hold and ordered groups of slaves to come up on deck. There, they received a breakfast of beans. This was followed by a practice known as "dancing the slave." As one slave provided the beat by pounding on a iron kettle or perhaps an African musical instrument similar to a banjo, the slaves leaped about the deck in a bizarre fashion. The purpose of the ritual was to give them exercise. Slaves were kept on deck to receive the benefits of fresh air and sunshine. But, come nightfall, they were sent below to spend another dreaded night of crowded existence.

Ship crews later remembered the horrible sounds of hundreds of slaves below, which included crying women, the moans of the sick, the wails of the dying. Their circumstances led some slaves to attempt suicide by refusing to eat. They were often force fed by having a funnel jammed down their throats with food pushed into their gullets. Some slaves chose to jump overboard. So many slaves attempted suicide by this method, that sharks regularly followed slave ships across the Atlantic.

Review and Write

Describe the ways in which the shipping of African slaves to the New World was cruel and inhumane.

Test III

Part I.

Matching. *Match the answers shown below with the statements given above. Place the letters of the correct answers in the spaces below.*

1. This New England colony was established when Roger Williams received charter in 1644
2. This framework for Connecticut's government gave men the right to vote, even non-churchmen
3. Early settlers in this colony were dissidents; Charles II granted colonial charter in 1679
4. Grassy meadow which dominated the center of many New England towns
5. Pattern of New England village settlement
6. Indian leader of the Wampanoags during war against New England English in 1670s
7. Wampanoag chief who convinced Miles Standish to attack the Massachusetts Indians
8. Southern colony founded in 1663 which was named after Charles II
9. Label given colonies founded by Charles II after the reestablishment of English monarchy
10. Name of wars fought between Iroquois and Hurons to seize control of fur trade in 1640s
11. Partner of Lord John Berkley who served as proprietor of the New Jersey colony
12. City site selected by this cousin of William Penn, proprietor of colony of Pennsylvania

A. New Hampshire	B. town system	C. Massasoit	D. George Carteret
E. Rhode Island	F. village green	G. Restoration	H. Philadelphia
I. Fundamental Orders	J. Metacom	K. Carolina	L. Beaver

1. ____ 2. ____ 3. ____ 4. ____ 5. ____ 6. ____ 7. ____ 8. ____ 9. ____ 10. ____ 11. ____ 12. ____

Part II.

Matching. *Match the answers shown below with the statements given above. Place the letters of the correct answers in the spaces below.*

1. European nationality who introduced the log cabin to North America
2. Native Americans who occupied modern-day Delaware before the arrival of Europeans
3. Name of Swedish trading post built along Delaware River in late 1630s
4. Original name for Georgia colony, given to the region by Robert Montgomery
5. Founder of the colony of Georgia, he was an English social reformer
6. Caribbean island that became an important English sugar colony after 1655
7. Caribbean island that became an important Spanish sugar colony after end of 16th century
8. This English sea captain was one of first to deliver cargo of African slaves to New World
9. African trade town which connected with Muslim trade caravans from the East
10. Name for African slave-catching raids
11. Royal permission from the king of Spain to import slaves to the New World
12. Leg in international trade which delivered African slaves to New World

A. James Oglethorpe	B. Fort Christina	C. Cuba	D. Timbuktu
E. Leni-Lenape	F. Jamaica	G. panyarings	H. asiento
I. Swedes	J. Azilia	K. John Hawkins	L. Middle Passage

1. ____ 2. ____ 3. ____ 4. ____ 5. ____ 6. ____ 7. ____ 8. ____ 9. ____ 10. ____ 11. ____ 12. ____

Creating Slavery in the Colonies

Once the slave ships completed the Middle Passage from Africa to the Americas, they landed in one of dozens of possible New World ports. For those who were eventually bought for service in the British colonies of North America, they found themselves facing a world they did not understand.

Most slaves never arrived in North America. The majority worked sugar mills and plantations, as well as many other types of difficult labor in the Caribbean, Mexico, or Brazil. Since the founding of the British colonies was not completed until the early 1700s, the number of slaves brought to those colonies remained low until later in the 18th century. In 1700, the number of slaves in British North America constituted about 11 percent of the total colonial population. By the Revolutionary War (1775–1781), however, the number of slaves had nearly doubled, comprising 20 percent of the total colonial population.

Slavery in the New World was over a century old before the first African workers were introduced to the British colonies of North America. Jamestown saw the first imports of Africans, when, in 1619, a Dutch warship docked and traded "20 and odd Negroes" for some supplies the crew desperately needed.

These earliest African arrivals, however, were not, by definition, true slaves. Since the institution of slavery did not exist by law in Jamestown, the Africans were considered yet another group of workers. These blacks were not thought of much differently than indentured servants. In fact, they and their children obtained land in time and eventually gained their complete freedom after paying off their passage to America. (Never mind they had not chosen to come to America in the first place.)

In fact, some of the early black arrivals to Jamestown would later not only become land owners, but slave owners, as well. And, only a few decades would pass after the arrival of Africans in 1619 before the laws of the colony of Virginia created the institution of slavery and defined it as a system of lifelong work.

The numbers of black workers in America did not increase dramatically throughout most of the 1600s. Since slaves cost twice as much as indentured servants, there was little economic incentive for Virginians to purchase black workers. As long as a viable number of white indentured workers continued to stream into the British colonies, the number of black workers—whether slave or servant by definition—remained limited.

But the availability of indentured servants began to decrease in the late 1600s and into the 1700s. Better economic times in England brought fewer young people anxious to come to America who did not have the money to pay their own way. Also, indentured servants were living longer, surviving their indentures. During the late 1600s, social conflicts, such as Bacon's Rebellion in the 1670s, which was led by former indentured servants in Virginia, led some planters to turn increasingly to black workers over a dwindling number of available indentured servants.

By 1700, the number of black workers outnumbered indentured servants. In the southern colonies, the percentage of the population that included blacks was much higher than in the northern colonies. In the Tidewater region, which included Virginia and Maryland, nearly one out of every five persons was black, while in South Carolina the rate was twice as high.

Review and Write

1. What was the labor status of the first blacks brought to the North American colonies of the British?

2. Why did colonists make increasing use of black workers as opposed to indentured workers? In other words, what made the system of indentured servitude no longer as viable or appealing as the use of black slaves?

Slavery Takes Root in the Colonies

Long before the end of the 17th century, the status of African workers in the colonies had begun to change. Racial attitudes developed which caused whites to redefine the role and definition of the black workers in the British colonies of North America. The southern colonies led the way.

In 1662, the Virginia House of Burgesses acknowledged the new status by voting that the children of slave mothers inherited their mother's status, meaning they would be born into slavery. Seven years later, Virginia leaders determined that if a master "accidentally" killed a slave while being punished, it would not be counted as a serious crime against the slave master. A generation later, in 1705, the colonial legislature enacted a comprehensive Slave Code which further defined the duties of slaves, closing nearly every door that might have allowed a black worker to become free.

Other colonies followed Virginia's example. With the institution of slavery more clearly defined and the number of white indentured servants declining, the numbers of black slaves increased significantly. While many were worked as farmers and field hands, the slave economy was different from one region to another. Generally, slaves were few in the northern colonies—those north of Maryland. But in the southern colonies, slavery became a widespread institution.

In the Tidewater region of the Chesapeake, slavery grew considerably in the 18th century. Eighty thousand Africans were imported to Virginia and Maryland between 1700 and 1770. But a greater number developed by natural increase—meaning slave couples producing children of their own. In fact, the British colonies of North America were the first in the Americas to develop slave populations that grew without constant additional imports of fresh slaves to the colonies. Natural increase could occur in the North American colonies, because slaves were never considered expendable, as they were in the Caribbean islands or in South America, where sugar profits paid for new slaves every four or five years. By the time of the American Revolution (1770s), the majority of slaves in America had been born there.

In the Tidewater region, many slaves worked in the tobacco fields. Tobacco was the region's cash crop. It grew as short, brown plants which were highly susceptible to weeds. Slaves spent many hours engaged in back-breaking labor, such as hoeing weeds.

While tobacco was grown in the Lower South, as well, slaves often worked the rice fields where that grain had become extremely popular by 1715. Many slaves from West Africa brought rice-growing skills with them, as well as a tradition of cattle grazing. By the 1740s, another crop became important in South Carolina when it was introduced by a young South Carolina woman named Eliza Lucas Pinckney. She was the daughter of a plantation-owning British army officer. Eliza was known for her agricultural experiments on her father's plantation, testing the possibilities of growing ginger, flax, cotton, even silk.

But her introduction of a plant called indigo was her greatest success. Indigo was a bushy plant which produced little sausage-shaped pods from which growers could extract a deep blue dye. Three years after Eliza's introduction of the plant, South Carolina exported 100,000 pounds of indigo.

Such successes caused slavery to expand in the Lower South. By 1770, 90,000 African slaves lived in this southern region.

Seven Colonial Regions

Students of Colonial America sometimes view the entire era with the same eyes, whether looking at 1610 or1760. But the colonial experience did not remain the same throughout two centuries of human experience. Thinking of the period as just that—one long era—requires that one ignore the differences brought about by each passing decade or even century.

By the mid-1700s, all 13 of the British colonies of North America had been founded. Life in these colonies had settled into a pattern and even a routine for many of those living from Massachusetts to Georgia. Many of the problems faced by earlier colonists—wilderness, starvation, disease, the unknown—had vanished by the mid-1700s, and, in some colonies, long before that.

Colonial regions were clearly defined by this time, delineated by differences which made each region unique. Historians identify at least seven North American regions that existed side by side by the mid-18th century. They were: 1) Native America, 2) Spanish America, 3) French Northlands, 4) New England, 5) Middle Colonies, 6) the South, and 7) the Frontier Backcountry.

Within the seven, three European powers, still present in significant numbers in North America, are identified: Spain, France, and Great Britain. In addition, the Indians of North America are also a significant presence in the 18th century. These seven regions reveal the tapestry of peoples who had come to live in North America.

First, a look at the Indians of 18th-century North America reveals a continuing presence of power. Through European contact, the lives of Native Americans living along the Atlantic coast, the Gulf of Mexico, the Mississippi river valley, the Spanish Southwest, and much of French Canada had been significantly changed.

Through trade with Europeans, Indians gained access to new technologies, economies, religions, foods, and skills. Those Indians living along the Atlantic coastlands became active traders in fur for which they gained guns, iron kettles, French trading

axes, and a host of other life-altering goods from the Old World.

These Native Americans typically allied themselves with either the French, British, Dutch, or Spanish, which brought them into European conflicts, just as Europeans were sometimes dragged into wars between Indian tribes who were traditional enemies before the first European arrivals.

Significant Indian wars had brought upheaval to native cultures. Sometimes, whole tribes were wiped out during such conflicts, such as the French destruction of the Natchez in 1731. Such wars were often over land and who would control it. Typically, Native Americans lost many of their tribal homes following the arrival of the Europeans. But warfare did not impact the lives of Native Americans as significantly as did the introduction of European diseases to the New World.

No accurate count of Native American populations was attempted in North America prior to the 1800s, but historians estimate that the Indian population of North America (the lands north of Mexico) prior to 1500 probably stood between 7 and 10 million. By the end of the 1700s, after 300 years of European contact, the native population had dropped to around 1 million. Most of these losses were felt by coastal tribes where the death rate following a century of contact with Europeans often ran as high as 50 percent. Yet many of the interior tribes—especially those living on the Great Plains—had not yet felt the impact of living alongside the peoples from the Old World.

Spanish America

While the heart of the Spanish Empire in the New World had always been located in the Caribbean and, slightly later, the Vice-royalty of Mexico, the long arm of Spanish influence found its way to North America less than a half century after Columbus.

By the mid-18th century, Spain still occupied portions of North America, most notably Florida and today's American Southwest, stretching from Texas across modern-day New Mexico and Arizona, to Spanish colonial California.

Spain's power was more considerable in some North American centers than in others. By the 1700s, for example, Spain's presence in Florida was already declining. Only a handful of significant outposts were still in Spanish hands, including St. Augustine on the Atlantic coast, where the old Spanish fortress San Marco remained dominant, and Pensacola on the Gulf of Mexico.

The numbers of Spanish in Florida was so small, that they had to remain friendly and cooperative with the Native Americans of the region, such as the Creek and Seminole Indians. Slaves from British colonies regularly escaped to Spanish Florida and found sanctuary in St. Augustine.

Two thousand miles away, and far to the west, the Spanish were still the dominate European power in New Mexico. But the region was a poor one, and it was regularly ignored by the Spanish authorities ruling from Mexico City, located 1000 miles to the south. In 1750, New Mexico was home to 20,000 Pueblo Indians, the Native Americans who first made contact with the Spanish in the 16th century. By comparison, 10,000 Spanish colonists lived in the region.

One reason for the relative poverty of Spanish New Mexico was the extreme control of the region by Mexico City officials. Trade laws restricted Spanish colonists to bartering their wool, buffalo hides, deerskins, and pottery for manufactured goods shipped over long, treacherous wagon routes from the capital of the Viceroy. This trade was balanced unfavorably against the New Mexico

Spanish and their Indian neighbors.

The Spanish presence in New Mexico had a direct impact on the lives of Native Americans living on the Great Plains to the north and east. By the 1680s, southern plains tribes had gained access to the horse through the Spanish, often by stealing them. The introduction of the horse changed Plains life by allowing the tribes of that vast region of grasslands to develop the horse and buffalo culture for which they became known to Americans moving west in the 1800s.

To counter the threat of a French presence along the lower Mississippi river, the Spanish, by the early 1700s, built a chain of military posts, called presidios, in Louisiana. In addition, they established Franciscan missions from Texas to California. As early as the 1690s, Jesuit missionaries, such as Father Eusebio Kino, built mission outposts near native populations along the lower Colorado river.

By the 1700s, California had become a significant part of Spain's North American world. Having explored from the Gila River to San Francisco Bay, the Spanish built additional missions operated by Franciscans such as Father Junipero Serra. By the 1770s, a string of missions had been built at sites that would today be significant California cities, including San Francisco, San Diego, and Los Angeles. The latter became the largest Spanish town in California by 1800, with a population of 300 people.

Review and Write

1. By 1750, what portion of North America was under Spanish control or dominance?

2. For years, the Mexican colonies in modern-day New Mexico were poor. What was one reason for the ongoing poverty of the region while under Spanish dominance?

3. How did the presence of the Spanish in New Mexico impact and alter the lives of the Native Americans living in the region?

French Northlands

The French colonial presence in North America was just as scattered as that of the Spanish. While the English colonies were connected to one another, all hugging the Atlantic Coast, the French had established settlements from Canada to the Gulf of Mexico. In fact, they occupied a cultural region known as the French Crescent.

The French Crescent stretched from the modern-day maritime provinces of eastern Canada inland, following the St. Lawrence River, to the Great Lakes region. It turned sharply south below Lake Michigan, following the Mississippi to the Gulf of Mexico.

This entire region was dotted with French forts, fishing villages, fur trading outposts, Jesuit missions, and even towns such as Montreal and Quebec City. This French empire in the New World was possible through strong ties with a variety of Native American tribes and clans. Long-term alliances and trade agreements were the common thread of connection between the French and the Indians.

The strength of the French in North America was not based on an extensive European population, as was the case with the British Atlantic colonies, which, by the mid-1700s, numbered nearly 1.2 million. At the turn of the century, in 1700, the French population in North America stood at only 15,000. Even as late as 1750, the population of New France had increased to only 70,000.

While the British colonies had created significant urban centers throughout the colonial period, such was not the case with the French. They had always been spread out thinly across a vast expanse of territory. The French had produced little domestic industry, as well, again unlike the British. The economy of New France continued to hinge on the fur trade, fishing, and farming.

A good example of a New France community was Fort Detroit located between the Great Lakes of Huron and Erie. By 1750, Detroit was a military outpost with a stockaded town. French authorities operated the community which included trading posts, several stores, and a Catholic church. About 100 families of French and metis, those who had both French and Indian blood, lived in the community where they farmed along the Detroit River. In close proximity were nearly 6000 Indians of the Huron, Potawatomi, and Ottawa tribes.

Fishing had always been the basis of the French economy in the eastern region of Canada. The maritime settlement of Acadia was home to fishermen and farmers. Inland, fur trappers and traders, the coureurs de bois and the voyageurs, continued to tap the rich source of furs in and around the Great Lakes. They did so through a series of intricate alliances with Native American groups, many of whom, by 1750, had been trading with the French for over a century.

At the mouth of the Mississippi, the French had established a slave colony called Louisiana, where sugar plantations sprang up.

Farming was important to New France by the 1700s. The farming communities of the colony of Quebec and those located along the Illinois River raised a variety of grains and regularly shipped wheat south along the Mississippi to Louisiana. The sugar plantations built in communities such as Natchez, Baton Rouge, and New Orleans reaped high profits for the French.

The Catholic Church maintained a significant presence in New France. The bishopric of Quebec was established in 1674. Jesuit missionaries moved further and further into the Canadian interior, taking Christianity to the Native Americans.

Review and Write

1. The French and the English established colonies in the New World during the same centuries. How were the two countries' colonial systems different from one another?

2. Describe the population differences between the French colonies in the New World and the number of colonists living in the British colonies.

Life in New England

Life in colonial New England began in the early 1600s with settlements by the Puritans who established authority and government with direct ties to their specific ideas of theology and doctrine. As part of that beginning, the Puritan colonies of New England—Massachusetts, Connecticut, New Hampshire, and Rhode Island—were built on a plan that allowed a community of believers to become a community that held land in common, building their towns and villages around a common meetinghouse and their farms around communal land. But in time, Puritan control of New England would face significant challenges.

The Puritans, not known for allowing the religious ideas of others, would eventually give serious consideration to the idea of religious tolerance. This change developed from within the Puritan faith, as Puritans themselves challenged the tenets of Puritan beliefs. Such dissidents as Roger Williams and Anne Hutchinson were exiled from the Massachusetts Bay colony, only to become part of separate movements to establish believers who settled new colonies, such as Rhode Island or Connecticut.

But the divisions among the Puritans did not immediately lead even the dissidents to accept other religious believers, such as Baptists, or Anglicans (those within the Church of England), or the Society of Friends, known as the Quakers. For many years, in colonial New England, such groups were regularly persecuted and hounded by Puritans. Baptists and others were jailed, flogged, beaten, tortured, and sometimes even executed for their religious beliefs.

As the end of the 17th century approached, the era of religious bigotry in New England was drawing to an official close. In 1689, the English Parliament passed the Toleration Act which upheld that no government of any state had the right to determine what religion was appropriate and that all church beliefs are voluntary. This meant that the no government could force its citizens to practice any singular religion.

By that time, traditional Puritan theology had begun to face changes. Puritan congregations experienced declining membership (ministers referred to this trend as "declension"). The regular attendance at worship services fell off with each new generation of New World Puritans. Part of the problem lay in the change of status of Puritanism in the colonies. In earlier decades, Puritan membership was voluntary, one chosen by each believer as an act of religious conscience. But after the found-

ing of Plymouth and the Massachusetts Bay Colony, everyone in the colony was expected to be a member, without having experienced a personal conversion to Puritanism. A doctrine called the "Half-Way Covenant," created in 1662, tried to fix the problem by allowing members' unconverted children to join as "half-way" members, who were denied the taking of communion, but were allowed to experience baptism, considered necessary for salvation and church membership.

But such moves did not alter the ultimate decline of power the Puritan congregations, their ministers, and the colonial leaders who supported their church experienced in New England.

Review and Write

How had the support by colonial government in New England of Puritanism led to the ultimate decline of power for the Puritans by the end of the 1600s?

Growth in New England

Although the New England colonies were slow to accept the Toleration Act, in time, various Protestant sects were practicing their faiths in New England without fear of persecution. The Puritan church, known by the late 1600s as Congregationalism, received financial support from the Massachusetts colonial government until 1833. But, by the early decades of the 1700s, Quakers, Anglicans, Baptists, Presbyterians, and others had established churches in many New England towns and villages.

While the connection between church and state in New England began to decline by the end of the 1600s, the old town system continued on successfully. By 1750, there was little land left in the New England colonies which had not been distributed to various colonists. The number of Native Americans living in New England had, at the same time, declined dramatically.

By the mid-18th century, the New England colonies had also changed economically. While the first arrivals, including the Pilgrims in 1620 and the Puritan founders of the Massachusetts Bay Colony in the 1630s, had struggled to create an economy based on the exportation of furs, fish, and lumber, these same colonies would, in time, develop expansive economic systems which were highly structured and diversified.

Coastal cities such as Boston and Salem in Massachusetts, and Newport in Rhode Island, had, by 1750, developed their economies to include merchandising, banking, shipbuilding, and shipping. As coastal communities, shipping had always been important to colonial life in New England. As early as the 1660s, New England shipping to the West Indies had begun to develop as an important aspect of the New England economy. By the 1700s, over half the annual value of New England's shipping exports were bound for the West Indies. These ships carried a list of typical items produced in New England, including dried fish, livestock, wood products, whale-related products such as oil and spermaceti (a waxy substance found in the

whale's head which made superb candles), and cereal grains. Nearly all of the last three items listed exported by the New England colonies went to the West Indies.

Although the populations of many New England towns reached their highest levels in the 1600s, followed by declines in many by the early 1700s, those towns still provided markets for the consumer goods produced by New England craftspeople. While many a pioneer colonist had brought few manufactured items to the New World, the established colonists wanted more consumer goods to make life easier and their work more productive. Such things as furniture, clothing, and tableware saw an increase in demand with each passing decade of the 1700s.

Farming had always been an important part of the New England economy and it remained so in the 1700s. But more and more farmers found themselves going into debt in the 18th century, in part because they bought goods on credit. They needed more land for their farms, but little new land was available at that time. New farms were established primarily in western Massachusetts, to the north in modern-day Maine, and west of New Hampshire, in the Vermont territory.

Review and Write

What goods, services, and industries provided the backbone for 18th-century colonial New England?

The Middle Colonies

By the opening of the 1700s, the Middle Colonies were among those with the greatest diversity of population, the two largest cities, and the most progressive economies of the British colonies of North America.

The economies of the Middle Colonies were dominated by the trade, shipping, and merchandising found in Pennsylvania's Philadelphia and New York City. The merchants, buyers and sellers of these two urban colonial centers had created a highly productive collection of markets with goods funneled in from the Hudson Valley, eastern Pennsylvania, Long Island, and Delaware, as well as trade and agricultural goods from southern colonies such as Maryland.

The Middle Colonies dominated the "American" trade with other colonial ports and with the West Indies. Fields in Pennsylvania and other neighboring colonies provided grain shipments to other countries which were worth twice the value of all other export commodities combined. Those additional commodities included flaxseed (which was used to produce linens), iron, livestock, wood products, and potash.

The Middle Atlantic region had grown dramatically during the colonial period. By 1700, New York's population stood at just under 20,000; by 1760, its population was 117,000. Pennsylvania grew from 18,000 to 180,000 during the same time period. During the same years, New Jersey grew from 14,000 to 93,000, while Delaware mushroomed from 2,500 to 33,000. New towns developed to accommodate the burgeoning population. From 1740 to 1770, over 50 new towns were established in the Middle Colonies.

Even during the 1700s, traffic problems in cities such as New York and Philadelphia were becoming legendary. An unwary pedestrian might be stampeded by runaway horses pulling careening wagons. The cartmen (colonial America's answer to the modern urban delivery men) wove in and out of other horse-drawn traffic, sometimes racing other carters, with all parties typically swearing loudly as they sped down the main thoroughfares of the cities. Accidents were plentiful, and, in winter, sleighs regularly crashed into one another.

The populations of all the Middle Colonies were extremely diversified. New York City was home to entire neighborhoods of people of the same ethnic background: Flatbush was home to the Dutch; Huguenots (French Protestants) lived in New Rochelle; Bergen County contained the Flemish; while the Scots settled in Perth Amboy. Black slaves were numerous, accounting for about 15 percent of the residents of the lower Hudson Valley. Many Germans lived in Pennsylvania.

Religious toleration in the Middle Colonies allowed for much diversity as Catholics, Quakers, Congregationalists (the descendants of the Puritans), Baptists, Mennonites, Jews, and others practiced their religious convictions without persecution. Most German immigrants were either Lutherans or Calvinists.

Government in the Middle Colonies provided a symbolic stabilization for the region. Farmers who owned their own property elected their own local government officials, including justices of the peace, which helped create tight bonds between neighbors. But these colonial communities still remained fluid, as its population moved frequently. During the 1700s, approximately half of the families of the Middle Colonies moved each decade.

Review and Write

1. What types of problems did one already find on the streets of such 18th-century colonial cities as Philadelphia and New York?

2. What served as the basis of the economic system of the Middle Colonies by the opening of the 1700s?

3. How were some neighborhoods in colonial New York City settled by people of various ethnic and racial blocks?

Frontier Back Country

During much of the colonial period, the settlers in North America lived close to the Atlantic Coast. They rarely ventured very far to the west for practical reasons. As early colonies, there was a need for those who migrated to America to remain within the vicinity of ocean-going ships, so they could receive regular deliveries of supplies and remain connected to Europe. Without such connections, it would have been impossible for the early settlers to have survived at all.

Also, early colonization needed to be able to sell its produce, whether it was tobacco, lumber, furs, livestock, rum, or foodstuffs. For that reason, connections with European traders and shippers was a must. But with the passage of time and with the consolidation of the English colonists into other successful ventures, there was a tendency for the colonists to move further inland, away from immediate access to the Atlantic. Part of this movement was necessitated by the lack of available farmland. The earliest colonists found land in abundance, and they grabbed up as much of it as they possibly could. This meant that colonists arriving later—especially those arriving between 1650 and 1750—often could not find available land along the Atlantic seaboard. They were forced to move inland.

But how far? And in what direction? A look at a map of the English colonies begins to provide an explanation. Nearly all of the land that was the original thirteen colonies was heavily wooded. There were few roads connecting the colonies, running north and south. This was due in part because of the difficulty in constructing roads or highways during this period. One problem in developing an extensive road system was the numerous rivers which typically ran from west to east, cutting across the path of possible intercolonial land routes. The rivers flowed to the east because of the mountain range called the Appalachians. These low-lying mountains—actually a series of ridges—cut across the colonies diagonally from New York through Georgia. The land to the east of

the Appalachians slopes abruptly, creating a natural landform called the Fall Line. The line can be found running from New York City to Atlanta, Georgia. The line is marked by rapids and waterfalls. It also serves as the furthest point inland that an ocean-going vessel of the period could travel upstream.

Bridge building was rare in America. In fact, as late as the 1770s, there were no bridges across any major rivers in the English colonies. The result was the movement of colonists to the west in search of available land.

These colonial pioneers settled in the western portions of their colonies, sometimes as far inland as 150 miles, a considerable distance in those days. Many of these settlers were poor, perhaps having served as indentured servants, who did not have access to eastern land after receiving their "freedom dues." They "squatted" on land to which they had no legal title.

Much of the movement to the West began in the 1720s in Pennsylvania and Virginia. These modest people planted Indian corn and raised hogs, fished, hunted for meat and furs, and lived in log cabins. Their lives were precarious, as they attempted to scratch out a living far from the security of East Coast civilization. Indian attacks were real and a dangerous problem.

Review and Write

1. In what ways were the lives of inland pioneers of the early 1700s similar to those experienced by earlier settlers along the Atlantic Coast?

2. Why, during much of the period of British colonialism in North America, did the greatest majority of the colonists remain close to the Atlantic Coast?

3. What was the Fall Line? What were its natural limits and where was it located? Did it represent a barrier to western movement or did it make western movement easier?

Southern Colonies

By the mid-1700s, the British colonial south was comprised of two regions: the Chesapeake or Tidewater South and the Lower South. The oldest southern colonies were those of the Chesapeake, which included Virginia and Maryland. The Lower South colonies were the Carolinas and Georgia. More than a century had passed between the founding of Virginia's Jamestown and the establishment of Georgia as a colonial enterprise.

The South of the 1700s was a region dominated by three racial groups: whites, most of whom were of English descent, but which included various European groups such as Germans, Austrians, Scots, Irish, Welsh, and French; blacks, the majority of whom were slaves held in bondage for the length of their lives; and Indians, those original inhabitants of the Atlantic Coastal region that still lived on the fringe of colonial society, who traded with whites just as their ancestors had in the early 1600s.

Of the racial groups living in the South, black slaves constituted 40 percent of the region's population by 1750. Ironically, nearly all of these slaves were forced to America, while the largest majority of the whites in the South were there by choice, whether their own or their ancestors.

While early settlement in the region had been along the Atlantic seaboard, by the 1700s, people had not only filled in the coastal landscape, but they had moved inland, following the rivers upstream, arriving in the great valley lands of the Piedmont, a rich farming country just east of the Appalachian Mountain chain. Nearly everyone lived in a rural world in the South of the mid-1700s. Cities were few and the standard pattern of settlement had resulted in the inhabitants dispersing along the river valleys, establishing farms and plantations. These agricultural outposts produced a variety of crops including tobacco, indigo, and rice.

In some portions of the South, the plantations were the most significant social and economic institution. By 1750, a typical southern plantation featured a large house, often set on a high place, dominating the surrounding fields and farm lands. Outbuildings might include a smokehouse, summer kitchen, barns, stables, corn cribs, and drying sheds for tobacco. Slaves provided the work force. Such laborers lived in primitive wooden cabins with a dirt floor. Such shacks were cold in winter and hot in the summer. Several families might occupy the same small cabin. Such "slave quarters" were a clear contrast to the sprawling mansion where the master and his family lived. Slaves referred to such a home as "the big house."

Despite the wealth embodied in plantation life, many white southerners were not rich and powerful at all. They were poor farmers who scratched out a living raising tobacco, since that cash crop could be raised profitably in small amounts. Such people typically picked up stakes and moved regularly since tobacco farming wore out the land within just a few short years.

While Puritan authorities had forced their faith on the people of the Tidewater region during the 1600s, English officials had established the Church of England as the official colonial religion. No other church was allowed in Virginia. All residents had to attend worship services, and taxes were paid to support the Anglican Church.

Review and Write

What aspects of Southern culture and economics explains why the South had few large cities?

Colonial Education

Education in the English colonies was a priority from nearly the beginning of the era. The Puritans placed great stock in the value of educating their young people. They saw a solid education as the means by which their children might make themselves better and help them become successful in their lives.

As early as 1635, New England colonists in Boston established a school patterned after the English grammar schools of the day. But education usually began at home. Parents either taught their children to read and write or they paid for some woman in the community to provide the service. Grammar schools remained accessible only to boys. In grammar school, young men were prepared for college. They spent much of their time studying Latin and Greek.

It wasn't until the establishment of common, or town schools, that a large number of young students were able to attend a school of any kind. Also known as "English schools" or "petty schools," students studied reading, writing, and arithmetic. Some of the early books used to teach arithmetic and reading were used for generations in the colonies. Several generations of Puritan children learned their ABCs by using the New England Primer. The drills also taught the young students important moral and religious lessons as they learned each letter, such as:

A - In Adam's Fall, We Sinned all.
B - They Life to Mend, This Book Attend.
C - The Cat Doth play and after slay (mice).
D - A Dog will bite, A Thief at night.

Other books, such as *The School of Good Manners*, offered instructions on behavior: "When thou blowest thy nose, let thy handkerchief be used."

Students practiced their letters and did their numbers on "hornbooks." A hornbook wasn't even a book at all. Instead, it was a small board with a handle with a sheet of paper placed over the board. But students did not write directly on the paper. Instead, the paper was covered with a thin layer of horn that was nearly transparent. Students wrote on the horn, keeping the paper clean.

In remote areas, such as plantation in the South, children were taught by tutors, teachers hired by their rich parents to teach private lessons. Older plantation children were often sent to England for further studies, including college. But by the early 1700s, South Carolina created "free schools," which were open to all children, except those whose parents were slaves.

Colonial schools did not include grades (such

as kindergarten through 12th) and students, regardless of age, occupied the same one room. Education standards varied greatly from town to town.

Colleges were established early in the colonial period. The first was Harvard, founded in Massachusetts in 1636. The purpose of a Harvard education was to train ministers. By 1651, this Puritan school boasted 50 students.

Other colleges followed. In 1693, the first college in the South, the College of William and Mary, was established in Williamsburg, Virginia. A tobacco tax provided money for its operation. In 1701, a Puritan minister named Cotton Mather established the college that later became Yale, in New Haven, Connecticut. (Mather founded the school after failing to become president of Harvard.) By the mid-1700s, King's College in New York was founded, which later became Columbia University. Chartered to allow students of all religious beliefs, one of the college's trustees was a Jewish rabbi.

Colonial Trade

When English men and women first arrived on the shores of North America to establish permanent colonies, they came with little support from English monarchs or Parliament. While kings and queens granted land titles to colonists authorizing new colonies, these ventures cost the English government nothing. At the same time, the early efforts to colonize cost many settlers dearly in both money investment and in loss of life.

However, even though the English colonies of North America were begun without any real help from king or Parliament, they still expected to gain something in the deal. In fact, every European power that allowed colonies to be established in the New World all anticipated some gain through the efforts of their settlers. From 1500 and through the next two centuries, every European government followed an economic policy known as mercantilism. (The term "mercantilism," however, was not coined until 1776 by English economist Adam Smith.)

The term mercantilism is easily defined. It occurs when the state (name any European power) directs all economic activities within its national and colonial borders with the intention of the state profiting first, followed by personal, private profit. In other words, whether the activity is trade, shipping, merchandising, exporting, or importing, the government must profit first.

In practical terms, the policy results in an expansion of national wealth by discouraging imports and encouraging exports. Today, economists refer to this policy result as a "favorable balance of trade." The English government, while pursuing mercantilism, allowed English immigrants to establish colonies in America so those colonies would import goods from England. The expectation was that these colonists would become consumers and rely on English markets to provide them with their needs.

However, this policy did not work well in America. The settlers needed desperately to export goods. North America was full of natural resources such as lumber, furs, and iron which required a minimum amount of labor. England, in reverse, had plenty of workers who could produce labor-intensive products such as clothing, fancy furniture, and wrought iron. Those two opposite conditions worked well to encourage trade between North American colonies and the mother country.

But to provide England with advantages in the economic system, Parliament passed regulatory laws limiting the colonies ability to trade with other nations. Such laws began to cause a drag on the economies of many of the colonies. Such laws were embodied in the Navigation Acts passed by Parliament beginning in the 1660s. English merchants pressured Parliament and the king to pass laws preventing the profits from colonial trade from going to foreign powers such as the Dutch, French, or Spanish.

The Navigation Acts of 1660 and 1663, for example, outlawed all trade with the English colonies except in ships owned and constructed in the colonies or in England. They also banned transportation from the colonies to any place except England or another English colony. A later Navigation Act (1673) required ship captains to pay a duty, or import tax, for loading specified goods in America. Such acts taxed colonial exports, provided revenue for England, and hurt the colonies. Such poorly placed economic policies helped sow the seeds of colonial resentment toward England.

Review and Write

1. While Spanish colonists received a high level of support from Spanish government officials when they arrived in the New World, was the same true for English colonists? Explain.

2. What was the economic system of mercantilism, and why was it important to the expansion of European trade and economics in the New World?

3. What necessary exchange took place in trade between the British colonies and England?

Part I.

Matching. *Match the answers shown below with the statements given above. Place the letters of the correct answers in the spaces below.*

1. European traders who imported the first Africans to Virginia's Jamestown colony in 1619
2. Laws which defined the duties and legal status of Africans in Virginia after 1705
3. Introduced the cultivation of indigo to South Carolina by the 1740s
4. Spanish fortress located in Saint Augustine
5. Jesuit missionary who built mission outposts along the lower Colorado River in the 1690s
6. Spanish order which built missions from Texas to California
7. Spanish word for military post
8. Spanish missionary who helped build and operate missions in California
9. Important French trade town in Canada
10. Natives of French Canada who were of mixed blood, including French and Indian
11. Another name for the Church of England
12. Term New England ministers used to note a drop in church membership among Puritans

A. presidio	B. slave codes	C. Eusebio Kino	D. metis
E. Eliza Pinckney	F. Franciscans	G. Montreal	H. Anglican
I. Dutch	J. San Marcos	K. Junipero Serra	L. declension

1. ____ 2. ____ 3. ____ 4. ____ 5. ____ 6. ____ 7. ____ 8. ____ 9. ____ 10. ____ 11. ____ 12. ____

Part II.

Matching. *Match the answers shown below with the statements given above. Place the letters of the correct answers in the spaces below.*

1. Waxy substance found in whale heads which made superb candles
2. Another name for French Protestants
3. Natural landform lying east of the Appalachians which runs from New York City to Atlanta
4. Name given those who migrated west and occupied land to which they did not have title
5. College founded by Puritan minister Cotton Mather
6. The first college founded in the South, in 1693
7. First English college founded in the colonies
8. Another name for colonial common or town schools
9. Textbook used by Puritan children to help them learn their ABCs
10. School book which had a handle and a thin layer of translucent material to write on
11. European economic policy which encouraged a "favorable balance of trade"
12. Outlawed all trade with the English colonies except in ships owned by English

A. squatters	B. Harvard	C. New England Primer	D. Huguenots
E. hornbook	F. mercantilism	G. William and Mary	H. Fall Line
I. Yale	J. petty	K. Navigation Act	L. spermaceti

1. ____ 2. ____ 3. ____ 4. ____ 5. ____ 6. ____ 7. ____ 8. ____ 9. ____ 10. ____ 11. ____ 12. ____

Colonial Government

Parliamentary policies, such as the Navigation Acts, were aimed at controlling colonial economics so as to provide support and revenue for England, even at the expense of the colonists and their livelihood. Parliament did not begin pursuing such harsh measures during the early years of colonization, however. These laws would have discouraged the migration of people from England and elsewhere to the New World. But once the colonies had developed solid economic foundations, both the king and Parliament began tapping the colonies as a source of revenue.

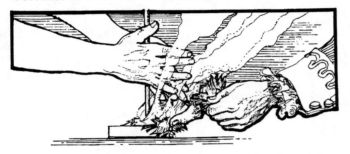

A parallel shift in policy occurred in the realm of politics, as well. From the early days of colonization and stretching on until the 1660s, the first 50 years of English colonization saw little political control wielded by either the crown or Parliament. These years were marred by civil war, the beheading of a king, national control by Puritans, and the restoration of the monarchy. England was too busy with its own political disputes to pay much attention to what might be going on in the colonies. (As already noted, Parliament did not make serious attempts to manipulate the colonial economies until the 1660s.)

This allowed the colonists a half century of settlement during which they were left alone to develop political structures and practices which were largely of their own design. Gradually, a pattern of government evolved in the colonies, based on a governor and a two-house legislature. There were differences from colony to colony. In New England, governors were elected by either the people or the colonial legislature. In the Chesapeake region, governors were appointed by the king or the proprietor.

In most colonies, a council, which was either elected or appointed, provided advice for the colonial governor. In some colonies, these councils served as the high court of the colony. In time, the councils developed into the upper house of the colonial legislature, while a lower house composed of representatives elected by white male voters provided representation for the colony's specific districts.

The result of all this political independence in the colonies was that, by the late 1600s, American colonists were accustomed to providing their own government and exercising a considerable degree of local political power. In some colonies, government received its power from the "consent" of the people in the colonies, a concept which lies at the heart of democratic government.

But, in time, the British crown attempted to limit this power of the colonies. Slowly, but deliberately, independent colonies became royal colonies, which gave full authority to the king over colonial proprietors and other traditional authorities. New Hampshire was one of the first to be declared a royal colony (1679), then Massachusetts (1691), New Jersey (1702), and the Carolinas (1729).

The most drastic changes occurred in New England in the late 1680s. England cracked down there, because New England shippers often avoided English trade laws by smuggling, and the Puritans continued to practice religious tolerance. In 1686, the charters of all the colonies from New Jersey to Maine were revoked and the Dominion of New England established, with the appointment of Sir Edmund Andros as royal governor. Andros dissolved all colonial assemblies. Andros was hated by New Englanders everywhere and became the target of a colonial overthrow. But a new royal governor was appointed and the move toward greater royal control over the colonies soon became another source of friction between the colonists and England.

Colonial Religion

By the 1700s, the English colonies had become a haven for a wide variety of religious groups. Although the Church of England was dominate in the Mother Country, America was home to many different Christian faiths, especially Protestant sects. By 1750, Americans had become accustomed to practicing their own religion and of tolerating the beliefs of others.

Several colonies had passed laws recognizing the rights of their people to practice their faith according to their consciences. While other colonies officially supported state religions, even there, Protestants, as well as Catholics and Jews, typically worshiped as they pleased.

Early colonial America had witnessed the significance of such groups as the Puritans and Anglicans, and even Quakers, but, by the 1700s, new religious sects were rising in importance. This led to a division among American Protestants between the "Old Lights" and the "New Lights."

Examples of the older Protestant groups—"Old Lights"—were those mentioned above. "New Lights" included more-recently established sects such as the Methodists, Baptists, and Presbyterians. The New Lights Christian churches were often more spirit driven, and more enthusiastic.

In America, Sunday meetings were common, well attended, and often significant social gatherings. Over 50 percent of adults in the colonies were members of a specific church, which they attended on a regular basis. Typically, churches were packed on Sundays. Boston's 18 churches provided services for its Presbyterians, Congregationalists, Baptists, and Anglicans. New York City was home to 18 churches, while Philadelphia had 20 meeting places. Such cities were dominated by the church steeples and spires which dotted the urban landscapes.

Just as today, congregational worship was attended by men, women, children and the elderly. Women sometimes served in significant roles in some churches, such as the Baptists, where they might preach, and the Quakers, where women

witnessed during meetings of the Friends. Some groups did not encourage the attendance of young children, however. Lutherans and German Reformed sects only allowed adults and older teens to worship services. In other groups, young children attended but did not sit with their parents. Those attending New England churches typically sat in the aisles or on staircases or in balconies. Any young attendee who acted up was reprimanded.

At the hands of the New Lights, America experienced a widespread religious movement in the 1730s and 40s called the "Great Awakening." This religious movement was intended to evangelize and rekindle the fires of faith in others.

One of the significant preachers of this movement was an Englishman named George Whitefield (pronounced Whit-field). During one whirlwind revival, Whitefield preached in nearly every American colony, preaching the necessity of being born again in Christ. His emotional appeal and great speaking skill swayed thousands. Another Great Awakening minister, Jonathan Edwards, preached against spiritual coldness, and caused his listeners to tremble as he delivered sermons reminding his listeners that God's mercy saves mankind from "hell's wide gaping mouth."

Wars in the Colonies

After more than 250 years of European colonization in the Americas, several key powers—most notably England, France, Spain, and Portugal—had continued as rivals over territory in the New World. At times, these powers went to war with one another. The wars were not often exclusively about colonial rivalries, however. Typically, the European wars of the late 1600s and early 1700s were simply extensions of conflicts which first began in Europe, then spread overseas, involving colonists in the New World.

One such conflict began in Europe called the War of the League of Augsburg (1689-97). The war extended to America where it was known as King William's War. While it was a war involving several European powers, in North America, it was a series of colonial clashes between England and France. Most of the fighting took place in the frontier regions of New England and New York. In 1690, French and Algonquian Indians attacked English settlements, burning villages of both colonists and of Iroquois Indians. The war ended in 1697 with the signing of the Treaty of Ryswick. In just a few short years, England and France would return to war once again.

By 1702, another war began in Europe called the War of the Spanish Succession. In this conflict, France and Spain fought England and its allies. The American part of the war was called Queen Anne's War (1702-13), after the English monarch. During the conflict, South Carolinians invaded Spanish settlements in Florida, burning St. Augustine. In retaliation, a combined French and Spanish fleet bombarded Charleston. The English emerged victorious from the conflict and, in 1713, under the Treaty of Utrecht, Great Britain won the exclusive power of transporting slaves to the New World. In addition, England gained control of French Acadia, Newfoundland, and Hudson's Bay

An uneasy peace reigned during the next generation, but war returned in 1739, centered in the Caribbean. The conflict between England and Spain was first referred to as the War of Jenkins's Ear (1739-43). (It was named for an English sea captain named Jenkins who had an ear cut off by Spanish officials in the Caribbean.)

By 1744, the war involved additional European powers, including France, and the conflict widened in scope, to be known as the War of the Austrian Succession. The New World action shifted to Canada where England and France fought for control of Acadia and Nova Scotia. This part of the war was called King George's War. French Canadians and their Indian allies raided New England and New York settlements, resulting in the deaths of hundreds of British colonists.

When an expedition of Massachusetts troops captured the French fort of Louisburg on Cape Breton Island (with the help of the British navy), the tide turned in the conflict. The end of the war was generally inconclusive, and the treaty ending the international struggle largely returned things to their status quo. (The British even had to surrender Louisburg back to the French.)

Despite the recurring nature of these wars, the primary rivalries between England and France were never completely settled. One conflict followed another, treaties were agreed upon and signed, yet each war left open the possibility for future conflict, either in Europe or in the New World. By the 1700s, one overriding question remained between England and France which would lead to another armed conflict: Which one of these two mighty European powers would dominate North America in the future?

Review and Write

1. What was the typical pattern concerning European wars during the colonial period: They began in Europe and then spread to the colonies, or just the opposite?

2. What events in the North American conflict were part of the European war known as the War of the Austrian Succession?

Strife in Ohio

Although the British colonists had remained along the Atlantic seaboard during the 1600s, by the 1700s, more and more colonists were moving west. By the 1750s, France and England were at odds with one another over a significant portion of territory: the Ohio River Country.

This interior region of North America lay west of the Appalachians, south of the Great Lakes to the Ohio River. Many rivers flowed into the Ohio, including the Monongahela, Allegheny, Tennessee, Cumberland, and Wabash. Much of the land was rich farming country and portions of it constituted a hunter's paradise. Both the English and French had come to tap the area for its abundance in furs. Their rivalry over this fertile, alluring river valley would lead them into another war.

By the 1740s, one immediate cause for war was the organization of English land speculation companies. These companies, such as the Ohio Company, founded by a group of Virginians, were attempting to entice settlers to migrate over the Appalachians and settle in the Ohio Valley. To counter this new challenge, the French built forts in the region under orders from the governor-general of New France, Marquis Duquesne.

The linch pin of the region was the site of the source of the Ohio River. The river is formed by the joining of two rivers, the Monongahela and the Allegheny. Situated in western Pennsylvania, both sides understood whoever controlled the Ohio would have dominance over access to the region.

In 1753, the French boldly moved into the region, building more forts: first, Fort Presque Isle along the southern shore of Lake Erie; then Fort Le Boeuf, southwest of Fort Presque Isle. By 1754, they built Fort Verango on the Allegheny. Furious at such aggression by the French, British officials in the colonies began taking serious steps of their own.

In October 1753, Lt. Governor Robert Dinwiddie of Virginia received orders from England to deliver a message to the French, demanding they stop encroaching on land claimed by the British. He selected a 21-year-old colonial officer named George Washington to carry the official papers to the French. Although young, Washington was chosen because he had traveled through the region as a surveyor's apprentice.

Washington tramped through the thickly forested region and arrived at Fort Le Beouf where he was politely received by the French. But they answered that they were not prepared to leave the Ohio region. In fact, the French were already building a fort, later called Fort Duquesne, at the source of the Ohio River. (A group of Virginians had made the attempt first, but had been driven from the region by the French.)

When Washington returned to Virginia to report to Dinwiddie, little time was lost before the Lt. Governor sent the young Virginian back into the Ohio wilderness. Dinwiddie's orders were for Washington to take some militia men with him to occupy the fort on the Ohio. (Dinwiddie did not know the French had already taken over the fort.) It was now spring of 1754.

While on his way to the headwaters of the Ohio, Washington encountered a Delaware sachem named Half-King and a small group of warriors. Half-King informed Washington that 1000 French Canadians were already building Fort Duquesne. He spoke of his hatred of the French, claiming they had boiled and eaten his father. He also told the young lieutenant colonel of the nearby presence of 32 French soldiers. Washington immediately decided to attack the unsuspecting French, a move which would later prove to be a costly mistake.

Review and Write

1. By the 1750s, both the British and the French were laying serious claims to the region known as the Ohio River Country. Describe where this region was located.

2. As the British and French claimed the same region during the mid-1700s, war would develop between the two nations directly due to what English move?

Washington Meets the Enemy

With approximately 150 men under his command and allied with Delaware Indians led by their sachem chief Half-King, Virginia militia officer George Washington decided to attack a group of unsuspecting French Canadians in the wilderness of western Pennsylvania. Still 200 miles from Fort Duquesne, Washington felt he had no choice.

On May 28, 1754, Washington and his men were positioned to attack. The French were unaware of the presence of their enemy and Washington ordered the assault early in the morning. Completely catching the French off guard, the skirmish went well for Washington and his men. Nearly all of the French party was taken prisoner. Washington only lost one of his men. The French asked for quarters and to be spared. Customarily, the young Virginian would have ordered the prisoners escorted back to the Virginia capital at Williamsburg.

But the day soon slipped out of control for Washington as his Indian allies began killing and scalping the prisoners. Half-King himself struck down the leader of the French party, Joseph Colon, the Sieur de Jumonville with a war club, killing him instantly. Before Washington could order Half-King and his men to stop the slaughter, ten Frenchmen lay dead. While he was able to halt the murders of 22 of the French, Half-King and his warriors were offended by Washington's actions, and abandoned him in the field. This move left the young Virginian with no scouts.

This was George Washington's first military action involving casualties. He later wrote with a young man's innocence about the encounter: "I heard the bullets whistle, and believe me there is something charming in the sound."

Following the French defeat, Washington pressed on further. He selected a site for a fort just 60 miles away from Fort Duquesne. He and his men had not yet finished the fortifications in June when Washington was reinforced by 180 additional Virginia militia. Fort Necessity was a dismal place, however, with constant food shortages. After about 100 British soldiers arrived, supplies were more available, but the fort and its hosts came under attack from French Canadians and their Indian allies on July 3. Many of Washington's 400 men were hungry and sick. He and his forces were picked off one by one as the French hid behind trees and other shelters, firing into the still unfinished fort.

Thirty men inside Fort Necessity were killed with approximately 70 wounded. Washington's situation seemed hopeless. A rainstorm blew in and doused the fort, leaving Washington's men with no dry gunpowder. The fort itself was reduced to a muddy disaster (Washington had placed the fort in a low-lying area.) That night, about midnight, Washington decided to surrender his fort. The French agreed to let the Virginia colonel return to Virginia with his men. The date was July 4, 1754.

As Washington surrendered, the French forced him to sign a document, written in French, which stated the terms of the surrender. Since Washington could not read French, he had no way of knowing that the papers he signed held him personally responsible for the killing of Joseph Colon.

Review and Write

From your reading of this page and the previous one, what is your opinion of Washington's military leadership?

Franklin's Albany Plan of Union

During the summer of 1754, in the wilderness of western Pennsylvania, young George Washington was defeated in battle by the French. But for the defeated Washington, the worse was yet to come.

The French claimed that Jumonville had been killed while on a diplomatic mission, much similar to the role Washington had served the previous year in delivering his message to the French. Without his knowledge, Washington had confessed to the murder of a French ambassador. Soon, the name of this future president of the United States became synonymous with villainy and treachery. Across Europe, Washington was not to be famous, but infamous.

Beyond the personal embarrassment and vilification which Washington experienced, the bloodshed in the wilderness was quickly leading Britain and France into another global war. As the threat of war loomed, the English colonies began to consider their advantages. For one, they dramatically outnumbered the French in colonial population. But they also had serious limitations to face. The English colonists were not accustomed to cooperating between colonies. In addition, the French and their Indian comrades were well-equipped, well-armed, and well-trained for a fight.

To bolster their strength, several English colonies began cooperating. In the summer of 1754, representatives from Pennsylvania, Maryland, New York, and the New England colonies met together in Albany, New York to discuss working together and to convince the Iroquois Indians to help them in their struggle against the French. While at the meeting, a delegate from Pennsylvania, Benjamin Franklin, one of the most famous men in the colonies, suggested a blueprint for cooperation called the Albany Plan of Union. The proposal suggested that the colonies form a council with the power to tax all the colonies. This intercolonial council would have been the first of its kind in the English colonies of North America. While, the men at the Albany Conference were able to convince the Mohawks of the Iroquois

JOIN, or DIE.

Confederacy to join with them against the French, the Albany Plan of Union was rejected. The delegates at the meeting were not yet ready to cooperate as colonies and surrender any independence to a wider authority.

In short, the suggestion to create an intercolonial government raised the possibility of a federal political system. But the delegates were not ready to adopt federalism yet. It would take another generation and a full-fledged war with England to change their minds and those of their fellow colonists.

War was approaching, however, and the British delivered several thousand British troops to America to fight the French. Those troops arrived under the command of General Edward Braddock, who arrived in Virginia in February 1755. While Braddock was a veteran of traditional European warfare, he had no experience with forest fighting, the "Indian" style of combat which the French and American colonists had long become accustomed.

In late June, Braddock set out into the wilderness to capture the French Fort Duquesne. He commanded 1400 British regular troops and 450 Virginia militiamen. George Washington served as their commander. Braddock's March was soon to meet with absolute disaster.

Review and Write

Why did the colonial leaders at Albany reject Ben Franklin's plan of union?

The French and Indian War Begins

Braddock's March into the wilderness of western Pennsylvania appeared doomed from the start. The British general, while seasoned and competent in European warfare, knew nothing of New World tactics. Nor, it seems did he care. He fully intended to tame the French beast, bring about the defeat of Fort Duquesne, and drive the enemy back to Canada. But none of these goals would be met.

One immediate mistake was Governor Dinwiddie's failure to provide Braddock with a significant number of Indian scouts and guides. Such warriors understood the enemy who were either French or Indian themselves. Had scouts led the way through western Virginia and Pennsylvania, they would have encountered hostilities first and given Braddock and his men the opportunity to prepare for a fight.

Instead, the headstrong and proud British general stomped and hacked his way through the region, marching his men in columns four men wide, while British axemen moved ahead of their fellow soldiers, cutting a road where none existed. Creating a road was a slow and tedious process, not to mention one that caused much noise. Surprising the French was, under such conditions, out of the question.

The French, then, were well aware of Braddock's advance. But they knew they could not remain at Fort Duquesne and defend it. The fortress was crude, consisting of logs and clapboard. It featured no corner bastions for gun emplacements, and there were few cannon on hand to use against the British. The French argued among themselves, with some wanting to retreat before Braddock's men arrived. Others argued for an ambush.

By early July, Braddock's advance guard stood within eight miles of Fort Duquesne. The British general's forces numbered 2500 men. His advance guard consisted of approximately half his total. Those at the very front numbered around 300 and were commanded by a British lieutenant colonel named Thomas Gage. With Fort Duquesne a few miles ahead, he made a terrible mistake. He sent his troops along a winding, snakelike Indian trail with each man following directly behind the other. Little did Gage know that the French and their Indian allies were waiting, hidden in the thick woods lining the trail.

In a surprise attack, 630 Indians and a few dozen Frenchmen opened fire on the unsuspecting British advance guard. Unable to see their enemy, the British regulars panicked and fled back down their narrow trail into the direction of their comrades at the rear, with their Indian enemies in hot pursuit.

Once the battle began, the Virginia militiamen, led by George Washington, took cover in the trees themselves and returned fire. But Braddock kept his men in the open, ordering them to line up and fire in unison, or in volleys. Confusion reigned among the British who fought against unseen enemies. Some British troops even fired on one another. Braddock was shot during the conflict.

Washington kept his cool throughout the fight, despite having two horses shot out from under him and enemy bullets ripping through his coat four different times. He helped his men and the British make a relatively organized retreat from the field of battle. Before the battle was complete, the British left behind nearly 900 men either dead or wounded. Braddock died three days later. His body was hastily buried and his grave site run over by wagons, so the Indians would not find it and mutilate his corpse. The first major fight of the French and Indian War had proven a disaster for the British.

Review and Write

1. As the English general, Edward Braddock, marched his troops into the American interior toward the French forts of western Pennsylvania, what mistakes did he make?

2. What happened to Braddock during the battle? What role did George Washington play during the brief, but bloody encounter

Montcalm Takes the Offensive

Braddock's men had died by the hundreds in the Battle of the Wilderness. Braddock himself did not survive his folly in marching through the frontier and fighting against Indians and French who hid from sight. The young Virginian, George Washington returned from the battle, along with many others, understanding the mistakes Braddock had made, yet he still failed to grasp the sense of loss, telling a friend: "We have been beaten, by a handful of men, who only intended to . . . disturb our march. You can see that life is unsure."

The war, known as the French and Indian War, would continue to go badly for the British after their loss in the wilderness. Over the next year, the French and their Indian allies attacked English settlements all along the frontier. The French further entrenched themselves, fortifying their new forts. On Lake Champlain, they had erected Fort Saint Frederec, which featured strong stone walls, a four-story bombproof tower, and 40 cannon. On the north end of Lake George, the French had occupied Fort Carillon (it would later be called Fort Ticonderoga by the British). Thousands of French troops occupied such fortress sites.

By 1756, the British sent Lord Loudoun to the colonies to lead the fight against the French. In the meantime, the French sent one of their best generals to Canada, a seasoned commander named Louis Montcalm. He was a slightly built, rather short general, but a man of grace and quick wit. His body was covered with scars, the result of battle wounds he had received on European battlefields. Montcalm, his troops and their Indian friends began attacking a series of British forts, beginning with Fort Oswego, located on the banks of Lake Ontario, which they burned in 1756. The following year, the French laid siege to Fort William Henry, on Lake George in northern New York.

Fort William Henry was a major British stronghold. Erected through the winter of 1756-57, it stood above the lake, commanding the landscape. The fort's walls were thirty feet thick, consisting of pine logs on both the inside and outside of the fort, and filled with earth and sand. A thirty-foot-wide ditch, or moat, surrounded the fort. A second British outpost, Fort Edward, had been built just 10 miles away, and a wide road connected the two strongholds.

For the siege, Montcalm had assembled more then 2500 French regular infantry, an equal number of Canadian militia, more than 1000 Indians, and hundreds of additional military personnel, including engineers, artillerymen, and boatmen. Inside Fort William Henry, Colonel Henry Monro had 1500 men, many of them colonial forces. As the siege began on August 3, 1757, the British and colonials knew they were doomed unless reinforcements arrived from Fort Edward. But help never arrived. The commander, General Daniel Webb, simply locked himself in his fort and never ventured out to give support to Monro.

The French followed the typical siege tactics of the day, digging zigzag trenches toward the fort's walls, and moving their cannon and mortars close enough to blow the fort apart. After six days of shelling, Monro surrendered on August 9. Montcalm offered generous terms to the British: All inside the fort could leave so long as they promised not to fight the French again for 18 months.

But when the French allowed the British to leave unharmed, the Indians were angered, having lost their chance for seizing prisoners and taking prizes of war. Once the British began the march to Fort Edward, they were attacked by the Indians, who killed 60 or 70 before the French were able to restore order. The Massacre at Fort William Henry was soon told throughout the colonies.

Review and Write

During the fighting at Fort William Henry, Montcalm approaches the fall of the English fort with a series of battle tactics. Describe how Montcalm brought down the English outpost.

Amherst and Wolf Take Command

With such French victories as the defeat of Fort William Henry and other successes, the French were able to gain nearly complete control of the Ohio River Valley, as well as the northern portion of New York. The direction of the war caused leaders in England to reconsider the future course of the conflict. In that light, a new prime minister of Great Britain came to power in 1757. His name was William Pitt. Pitt was a favorite of the people and often called the "Great Commoner."

Prime Minister Pitt made immediate changes in England's pursuit and strategies in the French and Indian War. He ordered additional numbers of regular British soldiers and more supplies. Pitt's new war aims included not only England's ultimate control of the Ohio Country, but the complete acquisition of French Canada. Should he be successful, the English colonies would become the dominant European presence in North America.

In pursuit of his goals, Pitt found the most capable military leaders and dispatched them to the Americas. One such general was Jeffrey Amherst. Major General Amherst brought the English victories. In the summer of 1758, his forces captured Fort Louisbourg which guarded the mouth of the Saint Lawrence River. By August, Amherst captured Fort Frontenac on Lake Ontario. These two victories gave the English control of both ends of the St. Lawrence.

British forces then turned toward Fort Duquesne at the headwaters of the Ohio River. British General John Forbes led four companies of Royal Americans, 2000 provincial troops, 1000 Highland Scots, and 500 Cherokee warriors on this campaign. As the British approached, the French burned the fort. The English rebuilt it, however, and named it Fort Pitt in honor of their prime minister. (The site became the city of Pittsburgh, Pennsylvania.)

By 1759, the French were reeling under the thrust of English military might, having lost control of the Ohio River Valley and of the Mississippi River. Then, in rapid succession, English armies took control of Forts Niagara, Saint Frederec (renamed Crown Point, and Carillon (called Ticonderoga by the British.) The Carillon campaign alone involved 12,000 British troops.

During these campaigns, Lord Amherst took no quarter with any French-allied Indians he captured, ordering many of their executions, mostly in retaliation for the Indian massacre at Fort William Henry two years earlier. The victories left only two significant French military sites intact: Montreal and Quebec, both located on the Saint Lawrence.

While Major General Amherst was responsible for many of these victories, another British general was rising to prominence in the ranks. General James Wolfe, after distinguishing himself during the Louisbourg capture, was given command of troops to march against the French stronghold at Quebec. Wolfe was relatively young, only in his early thirties, less than handsome, and often sickly. But he was a skilled combatant and a solid leader.

Quebec was the prize awaiting the British. Established by French fur traders in the 1600s, the settlement and its fort commanded the Saint Lawrence from atop high, steep cliffs facing the river. Strategically, the site was considered impregnable. The riverside bluffs provided great defense for the French. Also, the city was protected by General Montcalm, one of France's best. Any assault on Quebec would have to be well planned and well executed. Yet Wolfe made his plans.

The Battle for Quebec

The hypochondriac, but highly skilled, General Wolfe approached his command in North America with an open mind, informing his superiors that he was prepared to take up any challenge they might put to him. At one point, he wrote a letter to another officer, stating: "I am ready for any undertaking within the compass of my skill and cunning. I am in a very bad condition both with the gravel [kidney stones] and rheumatism; but I had rather die than decline any kind of service that offers." During the winter of 1758–59, Prime Minister Pitt gave Wolfe his orders: "Capture the French city and fortress of Quebec."

While the British already controlled both ends of the Saint Lawrence, they could not travel the length of the river, because Quebec dominated the river. Fifteen thousand French troops, under General Montcalm, were stationed at that key site. Wolfe's entire army numbered 12,000. But a closer look at Wolfe's men revealed they were among the best and the fittest of all the British troops in North America, while many of Montcalm's men were Canadian locals untrained in the professional arts of war. However, the French occupied the heights above the river at Quebec, and all they had to do was keep that control to continue dominating the region.

Wolfe began moving against the city in the summer of 1759. By late June, he placed cannon batteries on islands in the Saint Lawrence opposite Quebec. From there, they were able to pour shell and shot into the town, leveling many buildings. Next, British Admiral Sir Charles Saunders was able to bring eleven of his ships, including two 40-gun frigates, past Quebec, giving Wolfe control of the river.

From his new vantage position, Wolfe studied the bluff walls below Quebec. Often, he would dress as a regular soldier and walk up and down his encampment, studying every inch of the facing cliffs. His attention finally fell on a narrow, natural path which ascended up the cliffside.

He came to believe that, if several units of his Scottish Highlanders could be ferried across the river, secretly and under cover of darkness, they might be able to scale the 180-foot-tall bluffs, up this precarious, rocky staircase. Wolfe knew his men must act soon, or the river might freeze over when the fall weather turned colder. Once the river turned icy, no British ships could possibly maneuver. Wolfe planned the attack for September 13, 1759.

That morning, at dawn, Wolfe and his men began to move toward the cliffs. By 6 A.M., he and nearly 5000 men had climbed the bluffs and began to reassemble on the level ground south of Quebec. (The city was actually two miles to the north.) Once Montcalm realized, much to his surprise, that the British had conquered the cliffs, he exited the settlement and met Wolfe's army on the Plains of Abraham. Montcalm's move was a mistake, since his army could have withstood a siege laid down by Wolfe's forces. But now a fight was about to begin.

The battle was similar to a typical European encounter. Both armies marched toward the other in well-ordered columns, the British dressed in red uniforms, while the French wore white. Wolfe ordered his lines to charge, and Montcalm's men fired their first volley prematurely. The British marched on until they were only 20 yards from the enemy, then opened fire. The French line wavered, then broke, retreating from the field. Soon Wolfe himself was wounded twice. Montcalm, too, fell under British fire. Both men died of their wounds.

The French had lost the day and on September 17, they surrendered to the British. There was little question that the British would soon win the French and Indian War.

Review and Write

1. Why was the ultimate collapse of Quebec as a French stronghold one of the key goals of the English General James Wolfe as he fought the French during the French and Indian War?

2. As the battle for Quebec unfolded across the Plains of Abraham, how similar was the conflict to a typical European field encounter?

The Treaty of Paris, 1763

The battle of Quebec ended in a victory for the English over their French foes. The British had managed to surprise General Montcalm by approaching the city situated atop the Saint Lawrence River, after scaling high cliffs. Montcalm's miscalculation of the English cost him his life. Both he and the British commander, General Wolfe, were mortally wounded during the fight on the Plains of Abraham. It was the summer of 1759. By the next year, British general Amherst captured the only remaining key French stronghold in Canada, Montreal. The French and Indian War ended in a victory for the English.

But the war dragged on for another three years. It might have ended earlier if the king of England had had his way. In 1760, King George II died, leaving the throne to his grandson, George III. The new monarch was prepared to call for an immediate peace, but Prime Minister William Pitt intended to cripple the French empire. Pitt was replaced as prime minister, but the war continued until 1763. Little fighting took place in America, but the struggle went on in Europe, ultimately involving the Spanish as well. The European war was called the Seven Years War.

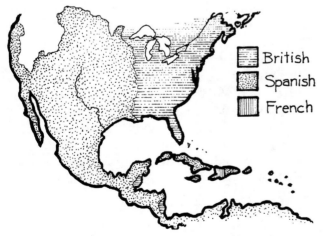

British
Spanish
French

Under the agreement ending the war in 1763, the Treaty of Paris, the British won great concessions from the French. To begin, France ceded, or granted ownership, of Canada to the British, effectively ending their colonial power in North America. In addition, Spain, an ally of France, gave Florida to the British. Although Spain lost along with France, Britain forced France to cede the vast territory of Louisiana, west of the Mississippi River, and extending all the way to the Rocky Mountains, to the Spanish. Britain was in no position to take control of Louisiana, yet the English leaders did not want France to remain in control of the extensive western lands.

The French and Indian War (the Seven Years War) was indeed a great victory for the British. But it came at a price. For one, the war had caused great strains between British authorities and the English colonists. Near the end of the war, the British had ordered forced recruitment of colonists to fight. This "draft" of American colonists was not a popular move. In addition, British troops had made a regular practice of commandeering wagons and supplies from colonists, often with no compensation, and had housed themselves in private homes without the colonists' permission.

Prime Minister Pitt became aware of the strains pulling England and America in opposite directions. He took steps to smooth over colonial sensitivities. He agreed to reimburse the colonists for any losses and placed the responsibility of militia recruitment in the hands of colonial leaders. Pitt also dispatched thousands of British regular troops to carry out nearly all of the fighting in North America during the late 1750s.

But the war had done its damage. There were constant and common clashes between regular British troops and colonial militia, at whom the British scoffed and poked fun. The fallout in Anglo-American relations went on for years after the war, and, for many, relations between the Mother Country and the colonies was never to be the same.

Review and Write

What losses did France experience under the Treaty of Paris (1763)?

Proclamation Line of 1763

The French and Indian War changed the balance of power in North America forever. The French were out, the English crown was dominant, and the colonists believed they were now free to move west into the Ohio Country without any threat from an alliance between the French and its Native American allies. But this expectation was not to become reality.

Indeed, with the French removed from Canada, the British were now in position to redefine power in North America. One of the immediate impacts of this new balance of power was felt by the Native Americans. While the French had paid Indians for the privilege of building forts on their land, the British occupied the forts, but refused to continue paying the rents to France's former native allies. In addition, the British did not treat the Indians as fairly in trade as had the French, refusing to provide them with free ammunition for hunting.

The result was Indian violence on the frontier. An Ottawa chief named Pontiac, who had been loyal to the French since the 1740s, turned on the British. In May of 1763, his warriors attacked Fort Detroit and other outposts. By summer's end, nearly every British-controlled fort west of Niagara and north of Fort Pitt (formerly Fort Duquesne) had fallen to Native American attackers influenced by Pontiac.

While the violence dragged on for another three years, resulting in the deaths of thousands of British colonists, the British ministry attempted to alleviate some of the problems between the Indians and its colonies. In the fall of 1763, the British Crown declared the lands west of the Appalachian Mountains to be off limits to colonial migration and settlement. This "Proclamation of 1763" drew an imaginary line from the headwaters of the eastern rivers that flowed into the Atlantic Ocean and closed the lands to the west, leaving them open only to Indian occupation.

This move by the British ministry was not a popular one in the colonies. Many had supported the British war effort with the anticipation of new

lands available to the west. Now those lands were to become a vast Indian reserve. Many colonists chose to ignore the proclamation and moved west, even at the threat of their lives.

In a way, this movement west formed a beginning of colonial protests against the leadership of Great Britain. The seeds of colonial discontent were sown in the victories won by the British through the French and Indian War.

That same war brought additional problems to British authorities in London. While the British had emerged victorious, they had also accumulated a huge debt in the course of carrying out the conflict. The struggle was a world war, involving tens of thousands of troops, scores of ships, and millions of pounds of equipment, arms, and supplies. The size of the debt was staggering. Prior to the war, the English national debt had stood at 73 million pounds. By the end of the conflict, winners or not, the British debt had nearly doubled, to a whopping 137 million pounds. Somehow, this debt would have to be paid.

But how? Where was the money to come from? By the early 1760s, the English people living in the British Isles already paid 30 times more in taxes than the American colonists did. With little hesitation, the English Crown began to eye the possibilities of making the colonies pay what appeared to be their fair share for a war that had produced victory on their own soil.

Review and Write

What was the British government's response to Pontiac's War? What new policy did Parliament create?

Test V

Part I.

Matching. *Match the answers shown below with the statements given above. Place the letters of the correct answers in the spaces below.*

1. Created after the charters of all the colonies from New Jersey to Maine were revoked
2. Served as royal governor and dissolved several colonial assemblies
3. Name given newer Protestant groups such as Methodists, Baptists, and Presbyterians
4. Religious movement of the 1730s and 40s in the English colonies of North America
5. English minister who preached in nearly every American colony the need to be born again
6. Preached against spiritual coldness and caused listeners to tremble through sermons on hell
7. Alternate name for North American portion of the War of the Spanish Succession
8. Name of an English sea captain whose ear was cut off by the Spanish
9. Virginia's royal governor who sent George Washington to deliver a warning to the French
10. Indian ally of George Washington's who facilitated murder of Frenchman Jumonville
11. Colonist who proposed the Albany Plan of Union in 1754
12. British general who led march of regular troops and militiamen into Ohio Valley wilderness

A. Jenkins	B. Edmund Andros	C. Great Awakening	D. Half-King
E. New Lights	F. Jonathan Edwards	G. Dinwiddie	H. Edward Braddock
I. George Whitefield	J. Queen Anne's War	K. Ben Franklin	L. Dominion of New England

1. ____ 2. ____ 3. ____ 4. ____ 5. ____ 6. ____ 7. ____ 8. ____ 9. ____ 10. ____ 11. ____ 12. ____

Part II.

Matching. *Match the answers shown below with the statements given above. Place the letters of the correct answers in the spaces below.*

1. French fort near the site of the British defeat in the Pennsylvania wilderness in 1755
2. French fort on the north end of Lake George; later renamed by British as Fort Ticonderoga
3. French general who led forces successfully against British, including against Fort Oswego
4. Site of killing of British civilians by Indian allies of the French following British defeat
5. British prime minister during the French and Indian War; Called the "Great Commoner"
6. Site of French defeat at hands of British soldiers outside Quebec
7. British admiral who brought eleven ships to bombard Quebec in 1759
8. New British monarch who came to power in 1760
9. Name for European part of war known in the colonies as the French and Indian War
10. Ottawa chief who attacked Fort Detroit in 1763
11. Parliamentary decision to set off land lying east of the Appalachian Mountains for Indians
12. Name given by British to former French fort; named for British prime minister

A. Pontiac	B. George III	C. William Pitt	D. Duquesne
E. Fort Pitt	F. Charles Saunders	G. Fort William Henry	H. Montcalm
I. Carillon	J. Seven Years' War	K. Plains of Abraham	L. Proclamation of 1763

1. ____ 2. ____ 3. ____ 4. ____ 5. ____ 6. ____ 7. ____ 8. ____ 9. ____ 10. ____ 11. ____ 12. ____

Grenville Taxes the Colonies

In 1762, Great Britain witnessed the rise of a new prime minister, George Grenville. One of his first responsibilities was to dismantle much of the huge military that had fought the French and Indian War and its European counterpart, the Seven Years' War. Since England was at peace, it did not need such a vast force of men under arms. He reduced the size of the army with one exception. Grenville doubled the number of British regular troops in the American colonies to 7500 men. His logic was that they were to continue defending the colonies, even after the French threat was largely eliminated. And he decided the colonies would have to pay for their support.

In fact, Grenville thought the colonies should be part of the answer to Great Britain's great national debt. Neither Parliament nor the monarchy had greatly taxed the colonies over the past century and a half. The new prime minister believed it was time for the colonies to shoulder their part of providing support for the Crown.

Grenville gave very little thought to whether the Parliament had the authority to tax the colonists. American colonists already, however, believed that they could only be represented reasonably by men they had actually voted for—typically, property-owners. But Grenville was of a different mind. He thought that the British government could legitimately legislate over the colonies, since he defined the "consent of the people" extremely loosely. Besides, Parliament had passed laws pertaining to the colonies for decades. Why should it be different for that body to tax the colonists?

The gap between the colonial concept of true government and Grenville's theory lies in the difference between the idea of "virtual representation" and "actual representation." Grenville felt the colonists, as Englishmen, were virtually represented by Parliament. The colonists saw it another way. Their concept of actual representation demanded that they physically vote for their representatives, just as colonists in all thirteen colonies did regularly with the elections of their colonial representatives. All the colonies had colonial assemblies with their members chosen by qualified colonial voters. From the start, then, this gap between actual and virtual representation was a key in the colonial response to British taxation.

One of the first acts approved by Grenville and placed on the colonies was the Sugar Act, which he brought before Parliament on March 9, 1764. The act increased the duties, or import fees, to be paid on various imports to the colonies, including sugar, wines, coffee, and indigo. Among other provisions, the act banned the importation of foreign rums and French wines into the colonies, forcing the colonies to buy only from British exporters. A significant goal of the Sugar Act was to keep the colonies from buying sugar from the French West Indies, as well as other commodities which colonists were regularly importing, effectively bypassing British traders.

Grenville also included in the Sugar Act the establishing of a vice-admiralty court in Nova Scotia and the deployment of ships to patrol colonial waters to search for smugglers. Colonial smuggling had become a lucrative business which allowed the colonists to import many goods and sell them cheaper than those regulated by British customs laws. Grenville believed that colonial smuggling was costing the British customs service as much as 700,000 pounds annually. The act was soon to raise a howl of protest in the colonies.

Review and Write

1. Explain the differences between virtual representation and actual representation.

2. Following the end of the French and Indian War (called the Seven Years' War in Europe) Lord Grenville dismantled much of the British military except in the American colonies. How did he change the number of British troops in North America?

The Stamp Act

The purpose of the Sugar Act, as designed by Prime Minister Grenville, was to raise tax revenues in the colonies, rather than strictly regulate colonial trade. The regulation on colonial commerce would have been nothing new. Previous acts of Parliament, such as the Navigation Acts of the 1660s, and the Molasses Act of 1733, had placed restrictions on how colonial shippers and merchants could conduct trade with foreign countries. But they had not been established purposefully to bring money into the British treasury. This difference caused a stir among wary colonials.

In addition, the Sugar Act's provisions calling for a vice-admiralty court outside the American colonies in Nova Scotia was only technically new. Vice Admiralty courts—courts designed to try cases involving accused smugglers, for example—had been in the colonies for years. But they had proven ineffective, were rarely utilized, and had cases taken from them by colonial courts, with the accused smuggler often going free. Grenville's plan was to put teeth in the court and to remove it from the influence of colonial courts.

Putting teeth in British law and its enforcement was important to Grenville's goals. It was time for England to enforce its old laws controlling the colonies and for new laws which would not only limit the power of the colonial smugglers, but raise revenue at the same time.

Such moves proved unpopular in the colonies. But colonial protests of the Sugar Act were ineffective. There was little organized protest. In 1764, eight colonial legislatures sent eight separate petitions to Parliament requesting the repeal of the act, claiming the measures placed great restrictions on colonial commerce. Also mentioned was the fact that no colonial government had consented to the passage of the act. But these protests were small, went unheard, and were of no avail. Grenville continued on his course of action.

The next year, in 1765, Grenville supported the passage of the Stamp Act. This act was modeled after an English law which was nearly a century old, requiring stamps on most printed materials. When he presented his plan to Parliament, Grenville addressed questions concerning colonial protests of the Sugar Act, saying he "hoped that the power and sovereignty of Parliament over every part of the British dominions for the purpose of raising or collecting any tax, would never be disputed." Intending to stave off colonial protest, Grenville suggested that the funds collected from the Stamp Act be spent in supporting British troops stationed in the colonies. The act passed on March 22, 1765, and was to go into effect on November 1.

The act required a tax be paid by purchasing stamps to be affixed on "every skin, or piece of vellum [animal skin] or parchment, or sheet or piece of paper." The law required stamps for all legal documents, tavern licenses, even paper dice. College degrees required the purchase of two pounds sterling worth of stamps. All newspapers, pamphlets, and advertising broadsides (posters) had to have stamps.

The colonial protest was immediate. Parliament had never created a revenue measure of such scope on the colonies. To make matters worse, the stamps had to be purchased with hard currency, or gold or silver coins, not paper money. Hard money was difficult to come by in the colonies and the Stamp Act would only cause a further drain on the American economy. Without question, the Stamp Act was a clear break with the colonial tradition of self-imposed taxation.

Voices Against the Stamp Act

The colonial protest against the revenue-raising measure known as the Stamp Act reveals several truths about the colonies. For one, they were not accustomed to paying taxes, so such measures seemed harsh. Prior to such acts, the average colonial citizen in America paid the equivalent of about $1.25 a year in taxes! Thus, an act such as the Stamp Act would have dramatically raised the tax bill for colonists, but the amount paid would still be a low figure, especially compared to the average taxes paid by people in England. There, the tax burden was 25 or 30 times higher! Colonial protests caused those in England to wonder what all the fuss was about.

However, colonial protests were rarely concerned with the amount of tax to be paid, but rather the legal principle behind such measures. Colonists continually spoke about their rights as Englishmen and how they had not given support to such taxes. They cried the phrase, "No taxation without representation," making it clear that they believed they should have a voice in such matters.

Unlike protests against the Sugar Act, colonists organized several types of protest against the Stamp Act. One type was the writing of political tracts, or pamphlets, identifying the offending nature of such acts. One such pamphlet was written by a brilliant Massachusetts lawyer named James Otis, Jr. His tract, *The Rights of the British Colonies Asserted and Proved*, addressed the question of Parliamentary power. Otis claimed that Parliament could not tax the colonies, since Americans were not members of the English legislative body. Otis's pamphlet, therefore, suggested that the answer to the question of Parliamentary authority was to give membership in Parliament to elected Americans.

Otis did not, in his pamphlet, suggest that colonists should not pay the Stamp Act taxes. He suggested they pay them loyally, but reluctantly. Other colonial protesters did not agree with Otis. One was a member of the Virginia colonial assembly, the body called the House of Burgesses. His name was Patrick Henry. Henry, a Tidewater lawyer, spoke against the Stamp Act before his fellow burgesses. During one of his more famous speeches, a student from the local College of William and Mary, young Thomas Jefferson, was standing in the doorway of the hall, listening. Jefferson later said he never forgot how Henry inspired him with his fiery words.

Patrick Henry also proposed to the House of Burgesses his Virginia Stamp Act Resolves in May of 1765. These resolutions were voted on by the members and five of the seven passed. (The burgesses returned the next day, however, and repealed one of them.) The resolves were a protest of the Stamp Act, addressing the issue of representation and consent to taxation.

Perhaps the most significant of the resolves was the one passed, then rescinded the following day. That resolution claimed that the members of the House of Burgesses held "the only exclusive right" to tax the colonists in Virginia. Already, colonial protests of such acts were seriously questioning Parliamentary power. And even though the burgesses voted the resolution down ultimately, copies of all five resolves soon found their way into the hands of colonists everywhere from New England to Georgia.

Review and Write

How did Otis and Henry view the authority of Parliament differently?

The Stamp Act Protest Heats Up

While fiery, colonial speakers, such as Virginia's Patrick Henry, delivered harsh words of criticism aimed at the Stamp Act, the most effective protest of the act took another form. During the summer and fall of 1765, with the clock ticking toward a starting date for stamp distribution in the colonies of November 1, colonists took their complaints to the streets.

In August, a group of Boston printers, artisans, and distillers called the Loyal Nine organized a demonstration against the Stamp Act. Early on the morning of August 14, protesters gathered and hung a dummy, or effigy, of Andrew Oliver, the province's appointed stamp distributor, from a tree on Boston Common. That night, a mob built a bonfire outside Oliver's home, and tossed rocks, breaking the house's windows. (They had already torn down a building they believed was to serve as the stamp tax office.) Thoroughly intimidated, Oliver publicly announced he would not collect the duties for the stamps.

Almost two weeks later, another Boston mob, calling themselves the "Sons of Liberty," rioted outside the homes of several customs officials. In their enthusiasm, they attacked the townhouse of Massachusetts' Lieutenant Governor Thomas Hutchinson (Andrew Oliver's bother-in-law), then looted and destroyed the home. Many people in Boston condemned the rioters for their actions against an official who, ironically, did not even support the Stamp Act.

Ultimately, these street-level demonstrations were copied in other colonies and became a fairly common means of protest. Other stamp tax agents were intimidated and convinced they should not perform their duties. Colonial governors announced publicly they would not support the act. Also, in the fall of 1765, about half the colonies sent delegates to New York City to attend a Stamp Act Congress. The colonies of New York, Massachusetts, Rhode island, Connecticut, New Jersey, Maryland, and South Carolina attended and produced a unified, but fairly mild written protest.

But the meeting was important, because it represented the first attempt at intercolonial unification since the Albany Plan of Union in 1754.

But additional intimidation was necessary to cause the British officials in London to reconsider the law and its unpopularity in the colonies. American merchants organized nonimportation agreements, or boycotts, of British goods and shippers to put economic pressure on Great Britain. It worked. The boycott hurt wealthy London merchants so much they convinced their friends in Parliament that the Stamp Act had to go.

So effective were the demonstrations and the boycott that, by November 1, the date the law was to go into effect, not a single stamp tax distributor would agree to complete his duties as a stamp agent. And, five months later, in March of 1766, Parliament repealed the Stamp Act.

Through a combination of actions taken by colonial legislatures, the organization of an intercolonial congress, boycotts by American merchants, and mob actions tending toward violence, the colonists had destroyed the threat of the Stamp Act and had questioned the authority of Parliament.

Review and Write

1. Would you have given support to the mob actions which took place as protests against the Stamp Act? Why or why not?

2. Who were the Loyal Nine and what role did they play in protesting the Stamp Act?

3. What act of violence was carried out by the Boston group, the Sons of Liberty, and what was ironic about their actions against the Massachusetts Lieutenant Governor Thomas Hutchinson?

4. What was the Stamp Act Congress, what did it attempt to do, and why was it an important colonial organization?

The Townshend Duties

Even though the actions of protesting colonists had brought about the repeal of the Stamp Act by Parliament in the spring of 1766, its members were not prepared to admit they had not had the power to create the act in the first place. At the same time they voted to repeal the Stamp Act, the men of Parliament passed the Declaratory Act. This act reminded everyone that Parliament had the ability to tax and legislate on behalf of Great Britain's colonies in America.

With the Stamp Act repealed, the question of how to generate monies in the colonies remained. The British debt was still sky high. So, in 1767, the British Chancellor of the Exchequer, Charles Townshend, used the Declaratory Act to promote new taxes on the colonies. His proposals intended to tax imports to America such as paper, lead, glass, and tea. But while previous trade restrictions had been levied on goods imported into the colonies from foreign countries, these duties, or trade taxes, were placed on goods coming to America directly from England. In addition, the purpose of these duties was to raise money, not regulate trade. Parliament went along with Townshend.

The Townshend Duties, as they were called in America, raised another storm of protest. (He also raised the ire of colonials when he suspended the New York legislature for not providing British troops stationed in the colony with such things as firewood and candles.) There were the usual pamphlets, such as John Dickinson's Letters From a Farmer in Pennsylvania. Dickinson, a well-known American lawyer, argued that Parliament had the power to regulate colonial trade, but not the power to raise taxes or revenues through trade.

Various colonial legislatures protested. Massachusetts legislators drafted a circular letter which they sent to other colonies. When British authorities ordered the letter recalled, colonial legislators refused by a vote of 92 to 17. The royal governor, Francis Bernard, delivered a harsh blow in 1768, when he dissolved the Massachusetts assembly. Other governors followed Bernard's

example, and additional colonial assemblies were disbanded. Since governors were royally appointed and they selected their own councils, the colonial legislatures represented one of the few bodies of political power voted by the people. And they were being eliminated.

For two years, colonists protested the Townshend Duties. The Sons of Liberty intimidated merchants to participate in another boycott. (Many merchants were enjoying booming times in 1768-69, and did not want to interrupt business again.) By 1769, British imports to Boston were down by 50 percent; in Philadelphia, they were off by two-thirds. Women joined chapters of the Daughters of Liberty, and held public weaving and spinning rallies, making their own cloth to protest the importation of British textiles. Colonists vowed to stop drinking tea.

By April of 1770, a new prime minister, Lord Frederick North, saw the handwriting on the wall and persuaded Parliament to repeal all the Townshend Duties, with one exception: the duty on tea. While many colonists were relieved by the moves in Parliament, some were unprepared to surrender their cause. The tax on tea remained a sharp, sticking point with colonial protesters. In addition, violence in Boston the previous month had ripped the city apart, providing additional steam to an ever-expanding patriot movement.

Review and Write

1. How were colonial protests of the Townshend Duties similar to those made against the Stamp Act?

2. When the British Parliament decided to repeal the hated Stamp Act, what additional piece of legislature did they vote to accept and what was its significance?

3. What were the Townshend Duties and why were they so unpopular in the colonies?

The Boston Massacre

On March 5, 1770—the same day that Lord North attended a session of Parliament to propose the repeal of the Townshend Duties—a violent clash between Bostonians and British soldiers erupted in the streets, leaving five American colonists dead.

The event soon became known as the Boston Massacre. It was a senseless clash but one which had been long in coming. For years, demonstrations against British taxes in America had occurred repeatedly, leading British authorities to station more and more regular troops in several major cities, especially Boston, the seeming hotbed of colonial and patriotic protest.

By the late 1760s, Bostonians found British troops—whom they called "Lobsterbacks" because of their bright red uniforms—intrusive and annoying. Redcoats stood on nearly every street corner, patrolling the city around the clock, stopping and questioning civilians. Commonly, young Bostonian women were subjected to insults and sexual remarks by the soldiers.

But the most antagonistic aspect of the presence of British soldiers in Boston was over jobs. British troops were not well paid, and a significant number took additional work to supplement their income. This meant that British soldiers sometimes competed with Boston laborers for work. On occasion, fistfights erupted between Bostonians and redcoats.

On March 2, 1770, several redcoats showed up at a ship-rigging facility, called a ropewalk, looking for work. A fight ensued. Stories were told and retold about the incident, causing some Bostonians to take to the streets. On the evening of March 5, a crowd of protesters gathered outside the Boston Customs House, and began taunting the lone British sentry on duty, private Hugh White, a redcoat known for brawling. The hapless White called out for help, and his captain, Thomas Preston, answered, along with six other soldiers.

Now, with a mob just a musket's length in front of them, the soldiers endured jeers, curses, and hard-packed snowballs. Captain Preston attempted to talk the mob down, but to no avail. Then, one of the soldiers was knocked down and, as he began to stand up, his musket went off. Other shots rang out, following his. (Perhaps, the soldiers, amid the noise of the mob, mistook their shouts of "Fire!" as an order. Street protesters often shouted the word to bring others to such a scene.)

Before Preston could stop it all, the mob fled, leaving five dead and dying participants. Three were killed instantly, a fourth died in short order, and a fifth, a young boy, whose curiosity had led him to see what was going on, would die later. An additional seven were wounded. Colonial patriot leaders wasted no time in milking the event for its full propaganda value. Rabblerouser Samuel Adams wrote against the soldiers, and local silversmith, Paul Revere, a patriot, did an engraving of the "massacre," carefully restaging the event to give the appearance of British soldiers, under orders, firing into an innocent crowd of Bostonians.

The soldiers went on trial for murder. Ironically, two patriot leaders, John Adams, who would one day be elected president of the United States, and Josiah Quincy Jr. defended the soldiers in court. Adams argued the soldiers had only defended themselves against an unruly mob. All but two of the men were acquitted; those two escaped with nothing more than a branding on their thumbs. But the Boston Massacre soon became a rallying cry among patriots.

The Tea Act

For nearly two years following the Boston Massacre and the repeal of the Townshend Duties, the colonies turned quiet. Few significant moves in Parliament raised concerns in America, and there were almost no violent encounters between British authorities and colonial agitators.

One exception occurred in Rhode Island where, in 1772, a British customs vessel, *Gaspee*, ran aground, only to be burned by local colonists. No one was ever convicted for the Gaspee Incident, for no one in the tight, patriotic community was willing to implement his or her neighbor.

But the calm that fell over the colonies was a superficial one. The dissolved colonial legislatures were not restored, and British policy of taxation was not ended. And many in the colonies were beginning to give serious thought to seeking complete separation from the authority of Parliament. Colonists were not yet ready to discuss true independence from England; rather, they were prepared to pledge their loyalty to King George III as the only legitimate British authority over them.

The false calm between 1770 and 1772 was shattered, however, that fall when the North ministry began to pay royal governors and judges in the colonies with monies raised from the revenues generated by the Townshend Duties. A newly created patriot organization, the Committee of Correspondence in Boston, was founded by Samuel Adams to publicize the British policy move.

Adams, a distant cousin of John Adams, was 51 years old in 1772, making him older than most patriot leaders. He had become by the early '70s a full-time political agitator. He wrote, called meetings, and organized patriot efforts often behind closed doors. He, James Otis, Jr., and Josiah Quincy, Jr. wrote a pamphlet that year in which they listed the rights they believed they and all Americans had, which included the absolute rights of life, liberty, and property. They also listed their grievances against British authority, including the use of colonial monies to pay royal officials and the forced housing of British soldiers in private, American homes. Such

writings helped to clarify the feelings of many patriots in all the colonies.

By 1773, the fires of rebellion were once again burning brightly and serious conflict marked British-American relations. In May, Parliament passed an act to give financial support to the failing British East India Company, a tea import firm. This "Tea Act" allowed British tea agents to collect the Townshend duty on tea (the only one still in effect) and return a portion of the monies directly to the East India Company. In addition, East India agents were the only ones authorized to sell tea in America, which gave the nearly bankrupt company a monopoly on tea sales. This would also allow the company to sell tea in America cheaper than the tea which smugglers brought into the colonies illegally.

Cynically, British authorities and agents for the East India Company believed that Americans would buy the legal tea over the smuggled variety, since it would be cheaper. It came as a great surprise when many colonists refused to be manipulated. Instead, dramatic protests involving tea occurred, the most famous of which was known as the Boston Tea Party.

Review and Write

What patriotic roles did Samuel Adams play in helping keep the protest movements alive in the colonies?

The Boston Tea Party

Although the newly passed Tea Act intended to bolster an important British company by selling tea in America cheaper than the smuggled variety, many colonists were not pleased. They interpreted the measure as a cagey way of convincing the Americans to accept Parliamentary authority, since the cheaper tea would still be taxed under the last of the remaining Townshend duty laws.

British authorities designated four colonial cities—Boston, New York, Philadelphia, and Charleston—as the first to receive the newly priced shipments of tea. As usual, Boston was the scene of patriot-inspired violence and protest.

The problem, once again, was not the amount of the tax on the tea that upset the colonists. In fact, the tax was so insignificant an amount that a colonist would have to drink a gallon of tea a day for a year before his tea tax bill would equal one dollar. The problem lay in the principles of power, authority, liberty, and legitimacy.

Three East India tea ships—*Dartmouth*, *Eleanor*, and *Beaver*—were ordered to Boston, the first, the *Dartmouth*, arriving in the city's harbor on November 28. According to the customs law, the duty on the tea was to be paid within twenty days of a ship's docking or its cargo would be seized by customs officials. Bostonians met all over the city in patriot gatherings and voted to keep the tea from being unloaded. They dispatched men to keep watch on the harbor and the waiting tea ships.

The royal governor of Massachusetts, Thomas Hutchinson, aware of the patriot moves, announced he would not permit the tea ships to leave the harbor. The days ticked by as the tea ships remained silent, bobbing in the hostile waters of Boston Harbor.

Then, on December 16, 1773, one day before the deadline for either the unloading of the tea or the confiscation of the cargo, 5000 Bostonians attended a meeting at the city's Old South Church. This was a significant number of people, since the city's entire population was 15,000. Patriot leader Samuel Adams chaired the meeting. During the boisterous convention, Adams made one final plea to convince Governor Hutchinson to return the tea back to England. The royal appointee refused.

Around 6 o'clock that evening, Adams announced that all talks were complete, and he could do nothing more to change Hutchinson's mind. This statement was a prearranged signal to the people, who began chanting: "Boston Harbor a tea-pot tonight! The Mohawks are coming!" The meeting began to break up, and the patriots filed out, heading over to the harbor.

As thousands gathered along the wharf, about 60 men appeared, dressed as Mohawk Indians. They forced their way aboard the three tea ships, broke open the tea crates and dumped the controversial cargo into the dark waters below. By 9 P.M. this "Boston Tea Party" had destroyed 342 chests of tea valued at 10,000 pounds.

When word of the tea's destruction reached Lord North in London six weeks later, his ministry ordered the closing of the Boston port. This was just the beginning of the harsh measurements which would soon be felt by Bostonians.

Review and Write

1. Why do you think the colonists refused to allow the East India Tea to be imported even though it would allow them to buy cheaper tea?

2. While the Tea Act placed a tax on tea sold in the American colonies, why did the colonial protest probably seem like an over-reaction to British authorities?

3. After the arrival of three East India tea ships arrived in Boston harbor on November 28, what significance did another date—December 17—have regarding the refusal of the colonists to allow the tea to be unloaded.

4. Describe the "Boston Tea Party" and relate the response of the British Prime Minister, Lord North.

The First Continental Congress

Following the Boston Tea Party, the British prime minister, Lord North, was furious. He chose not to seek out the instigators or the mob-inspired actions, but instead decided to punish all of Boston. By closing the harbor, he immediate hardship in the city. Sea-going trade was the backbone of Boston's economy. With no ships coming in or going out, North's moves appeared harsh to most Bostonians. (North did allow food and firewood to be shipped in, but that was all.)

By the spring of 1774, Parliament went even further in punishing Boston, by passing three punitive acts aimed at Massachusetts patriots. The Massachusetts Government Act increased the power of the royal governor and forbid all special town meetings. The Justice Act allowed the trial of anyone accused of committing a murder while attempting to stop a riot to take place outside the colony where the alleged crime took place. The Quartering Act gave British soldiers greater freedom to commandeer private homes and buildings to house British troops stationed in Massachusetts. While members of Parliament believed the colonists would have no choice but to accept these Coercive Acts, the colonists saw the acts as part of a deliberate conspiracy to oppress them. Events in America were reaching a point of crisis. What no one knew in the spring of 1774 was that a shooting war between American colonists and British troops was only a year away.

That fall, many of the colonies agreed to send delegates to an intercolonial conference to discuss the growing rifts between themselves and British authority. Fifty-five men met in Philadelphia in September 1774. Nearly everyone attending this First Continental Congress had been chosen illegally, since most of the colonial legislatures had been dissolved by various royal governors.

When they took up their issues, the delegates meeting in Carpenters' Hall realized they needed to focus on several key issues: 1) What were the colonies upset about?, 2) What do they intend to do about it?, and 3) Is it time for a new relationship between England and the colonies?

Great debates ensued, and the delegates could only agree on a few topics. Nearly everyone wanted the repeal of several Parliamentary acts, especially the Coercive Acts (in the colonies, they were called the Intolerable Acts). Most of the delegates were able to agree on a colonial response, choosing to petition the king and order another economic boycott.

The thornier question of a new relationship with the Mother Country was not easily addressed. Some delegates were conservatives who suggested it was time for the colonies to accept Parliamentary authority. Others suggested the establishment of an American legislature representing all the colonies, with the power to make laws. Such an assembly would still have to abide by Parliament's authority. More extreme delegates, including radicals such as Patrick Henry and Thomas Jefferson argued that the colonists need only recognize the authority of the king and to ignore Parliament.

What was not suggested at this 1774 congress was the idea of complete independence from England. Nearly everyone in the colonies, including patriot leaders, still thought a new relationship with England was possible, one in which the Crown would recognize the rights of colonists as English men and women. Independence would not become a political goal of many Americans for another two years.

Review and Write

1. Do you think the punishments placed on the people of Boston following the Boston Tea Party were appropriate? Why or why not?

2. When the delegates to the First Continental Congress met in Philadelphia, what three questions were on their minds?

Separating from Great Britain

The political divisions that were recognized among the delegates attending the First Continental Congress during the fall of 1774, made it clear that American colonists could not be relied upon to have an unquestioning loyalty to Great Britain, which included both the monarch and Parliament.

The decade between the end of the French and Indian War and the calling of this intercolonial meeting had witnessed a change in the minds of many Americans. In the 1750s, it would not have occurred to many in the colonies to question British authority. Men fought on behalf of their king and country, even though they had been born in the colonies and never even visited the British Isles. There was an expectation of loyalty toward the king or queen and nearly all those colonists of English descent thought of themselves as full-fledged English men or women.

What a difference a decade can make. By the early 1770s, many colonials no longer thought of themselves even as English, but, instead, as Americans. They and those who had come before them had forged a new identity. A spirit of independence, of social openness, or having the ability to work one's way up from nothing—these qualities had driven several generations to develop an "American" view of their world.

One aspect of that view was based on how the colonists looked at authority. Early on, colonists gained the right to elect their own political leaders, to make their own laws, to create their own systems of trade, finance, and shipping. Throughout the 1600s and the first fifty years of the 1700s, England largely left the colonies to pursue their own economic and political goals. Parliament might pass laws designed to control trade, but British authorities rarely enforced such regulations. Similarly, each colony developed its own legislative assembly, providing American colonists with a representation of their own choosing.

This independence from British control became a matter of course in America. Only when the British attempted to crack down on the colonies, by enforcing earlier laws and creating new laws constricting trade and commerce, did the colonies begin to feel the brunt of British authority and power. Only when British officials began dissolving local courts and legislative assemblies did the colonists begin to reassess their relationship with the Mother Country. Only when the British began placing thousands of regular troops on the streets of colonial cities did the people give serious thought to pursuing rebellion, riot, boycott, and other political mischief.

The colonists slowly, but with determination, throughout the 1760s and 1770s began a psychological separation from Great Britain which played itself out in a variety of subtle ways. By 1774, every colony was holding popularly elected provincial conventions. Royal governors and their councils were losing respect. Royal courts were less and less recognized. Militiamen ignored royal orders to muster and drill, instead responding to local patriot committees. And, perhaps, most importantly—by 1774, many colonists were refusing to pay their colonial taxes to British authorities. Instead they paid them to colonial convention collectors.

Review and Write

In what ways had American colonists changed in their relationship with England by the 1770s?

Voices of Revolution

By the 1770s, more and more Americans were making a psychological, economic, and political break from English authority. Sometimes these changes were clear and obvious, as when patriots supported boycotts, or threw tea into Boston Harbor, or tarred and feathered British tax agents. In other ways, the separation might occur in more subtle ways. However, the end result was a widening rift between many colonists and British officials.

Our chains are forged, ...give me liberty, or give me death!

Patriot leaders were often at the forefront of such change. Such men worked as political agitators, who stirred the hearts and minds of men and women throughout the colonies toward rebellion against British authority, whether royal governor, king, or Parliament.

Several key patriots stand out. One was Samuel Adams. Adams came from a prominent Massachusetts family. A lifelong resident of Boston, and cousin to John Adams, he attended Harvard College, then entered private business. He failed to prosper and fell deeply into debt by 1764.

While Adams was a professional failure (he later became the official junk dealer for Boston and lived in near poverty), he was to become a political genius. He campaigned against the Sugar Act and the Stamp Act, and organized patriot groups. The fiery Adams played a role in organizing boycotts of British goods sold in Boston, and it was he who gave the signal for the "Mohawk" raid on British tea ships in Boston Harbor.

Adams was elected to the Massachusetts assembly in 1765, and served until 1774. It was through Adams's organizing efforts that the first committee of correspondence was formed to keep colonists informed of British moves and policy. Adams was one of the original delegates from Massachusetts to the First Continental Congress. For a solid decade, Adams remained a constant thorn in the side of British officials, gaining him a reputation as a trouble-maker and rabblerouser.

Patrick Henry was another political agitator. He was born on a Virginia farm and grew up listening to his father read aloud from the Bible. Henry grew up to be a capable public speaker, one who could stir the hearts of his audience with the intensity of his words.

Henry attended college in Scotland, returning to America to operate a store which failed. He attempted farming and failed at that effort as well. Eventually, he studied law and became a successful lawyer and politician. (Henry also developed a lifelong love for playing the fiddle. Once, he and Thomas Jefferson, a fellow violin-playing Virginian, attended the same Christmas party where they played their violins while others danced country jigs and reels.)

While serving in the Virginia House of Burgesses, Patrick Henry was best known for his patriotic speeches questioning British authority. He was long remembered for speaking against the Stamp Act. After the closing of Boston Harbor, following the patriot tea dumping in 1773, Henry gave a speech denouncing the closing of Boston Harbor. "Our chains are forged," he shouted, "their clanking may be heard on the plains of Boston. The war is actually begun . . . I know not what course others may take, but as for me, give me liberty, or give me death!"

Without such leaders as Samuel Adams, Patrick Henry, and others, the causes taken up by Americans in the 1770s, which eventually led to revolution, might never have been given a voice.

Review and Write

How were such patriot leaders as Samuel Adams and Patrick Henry able to rally support for the cause against Great Britain?

Taking Sides in the Revolution

Even though many American colonists were inspired by the fiery words of Samuel Adams, and Patrick Henry, many others did not give their support to the patriot cause. In 1774 and 1775, American conservatives wrote against the drive of revolution sweeping the colonies. They published essays and pamphlets which criticized the efforts, even the existence, of the First Continental Congress, the committees of correspondence, and other agents of change. A lawyer named Daniel Leonard was one such colonist who intended to remain loyal to Britain and the Crown. In one of his essays, Leonard wrote: "There is no possible medium between absolute independence and subjection to the authority of Parliament."

To Leonard, the future relationship with Great Britain would have to be all or nothing. Ironically, he was one of the few speaking about independence (although he was opposed to it) in the colonies, even before its supporters found their voice.

Who was, by the mid-1700s, giving support to the patriot camp, and who was remaining loyal to England? It might be surprising to know. John Adams, one of the most brilliant and thoughtful of the patriot leaders, came to believe that the colonists could be divided into three camps, each one equal in size. Adams estimated that approximately one-third of the colonists were inclined toward the patriot cause; another third continued to support England as Loyalists; and a final third were neutral on the subject, giving no consistent support to either side and having no strong convictions on the issues which were already dividing the colonies.

More modern research indicates a slightly different spread. In reality, approximately 40 percent, two out of every five white American colonists (these figures would not include black slaves who often were not free to express a position or opinion) gave support to the patriot causes and to the approaching revolution. These people would rally, fight, and ultimately die for the revolution. They were small farmers who owned their own property; members of dominant Protestant sects; merchants and urban artisans, including skilled workers; those elected to office; and, perhaps, ironically, people of English descent. (Such people believed their rights as Englishmen were being trampled by British authorities.) Such people participated in boycotts; they wrote pamphlets; they rallied patriot groups; the women sewed to avoid importing heavily taxed textiles; and they took up arms against the British during the American Revolution.

Approximately 20 percent of colonists, however, remained loyal to Great Britain. They included British-appointed officials; merchants dependent on British trade; Anglican church (Church of England) members; former British soldiers who remained in the colonies after their service; and farmers who worked the lands of a British landlord.

Another 40 percent, a group just as large as the patriot supporters, were neutral to the events taking place around them. They either would not or could not give support to either side. They included Quakers, who were pacifists; and many Scot-Irish, who were angry at both sides for a variety of reasons.

Such statistics reveal that those colonists who actively supported the patriot cause were often in the minority. Yet they projected themselves and their ideas forward and brought about extraordinary change in America.

Review and Write

1. Which side do you believe you would have supported: rebel, loyalist, or neutral?

2. By the mid-1700s, the great American patriot leader, John Adams, believed the American colonists could be divided into three groups. Identify each of the groups.

3. What groups could be identified as colonists who were typically neutral in the American colonies?

Britain Prepares to Strike

Patriot efforts criticizing, challenging, even threatening British authorities in the colonies finally came to a head in 1775. The British king, George III, as well as his closest advisors, had become convinced that the rebellion underway in America must be stopped, possibly with a show of military force. Many of the king's ministers were certain that, once the British army came down on the colonists like a hammer, nearly all patriot resistance and agitation would come to an end. They were dead wrong.

Throughout the winter of 1774–75, British authorities began preparing for the destruction of the patriots and their strongholds. British general Thomas Gage, who was serving as the military governor of Massachusetts, received orders from British superiors to "arrest and imprison the principal actors and abettors" of the patriot-led rebellion. Such men included Samuel Adams and John Hancock, one of the wealthiest merchant-shippers in Massachusetts, who had once defied a British customs official by locking him in the galley of one of Hancock's ships, while the crew unloaded a cargo of untaxed wine.

In London, King George III and members of Parliament authorized monies to provide the dispatch of additional British regular troops to the colonies. Three high-ranking British generals were also sent over: William Howe, Henry Clinton, and John Burgoyne, known as "Gentleman Johnny." These experienced generals were intended to intimidate the rebels.

Massachusetts, always the centerpiece of rebel action, was declared to be in a state of rebellion. This status gave British soldiers the right to fire upon any suspected patriot rebel on sight, in an effort to quash the American cause. In time, this declaration applied to all rebels in all thirteen colonies.

However, violence had broken out much earlier between British authorities in Massachusetts and the patriots, however. General-Governor Gage had marched British regulars into the Massachusetts countryside as early as September 1774, the same month the First Continental Congress began meeting. His goal had been to uncover stockpiles of rebel guns and ammunition, rumored to be stored at small Massachusetts towns such as Charlestown and Cambridge.

But such heavy-handed actions had only strengthened the patriot fervor. As many as 20,000 colonial militiamen had mobilized against the British incursions to protect their military supplies at sites including Concord and Worcester. During a town meeting in Concord (an illegal gathering), those present raised two companies of troops who pledged to "Stand at a minute's warning in case of alarm." These volunteers were the first of the famous "Minutemen." Of the male adults from Concord, four out of five signed a document called the Solemn League and Covenant. Several single women signed the agreement, as well.

Under this document, they agreed to support the rebel cause and the illegally formed Patriot Government. Additional rural Massachusetts towns created and signed similar pledges. Gage found himself hemmed in by the presence of thousands of antagonistic rebel militiamen and was soon losing any effective support or power outside the city of Boston itself, where 3,500 British troops backed up his decisions.

Review and Write

1. What events described on this page indicate that the division between Americans and British authorities are swiftly coming to point of crisis?

2. By the spring of 1775, what decision had been made by the British monarch George III and his advisors regarding the rebellion of the patriots in the American colonies?

3. What serious steps did the king and his advisors make toward the colonies which could only result in an escalation of violence and conflict between British authorities in the colonies and the patriots?

The Focus on Boston

In April of 1775, General Thomas Gage received secret orders from ministers to George III that would change the course of history. Gage was instructed to arrest rebel leaders and, once and for all, end the rebellion in Massachusetts.

Thus far, Gage had been timid in his dealings with the rebels. He tried to avoid a clash of arms with them, and they reciprocated by repeatedly hesitating to fire upon the king's troops. Every time Gage's men moved, whether in Massachusetts or New Hampshire, they failed to produce results. This was partly due to an extensive spy network operated by Boston silversmith, Paul Revere, who kept his fellow rebels well-informed.

Gage's hesitations had given renewed boldness to the patriot leaders. Members of the Massachusetts Assembly (officially disbanded by royal governor, Thomas Hutchinson) had begun to meet again, based on their own authority and in defiance of the British. The House members voted to collect colonial taxes for themselves and saw themselves as the true government of the colony. They also gave support to rebel militiamen.

Such bold steps caused the Colonial Secretary of State for America, Lord Dartmouth, to declare the colony of Massachusetts to be in "Open Rebellion." His orders were added to those of British officials in London, giving Gage instructions to use force against this "rude rabble."

The general-governor's tasks were at once simple and complicated—to capture rebel leaders Sam Adams and John Hancock, who were rumored to be in hiding around Concord, and not to fire the first shot. If there was to be bloodshed, the patriots would have to start it.

Gage's spies informed him that the shortest and fastest route to Concord, located about 20 miles northwest of Boston, was along the primary road through the little town of Lexington. The rebels knew the British troops in Boston were under orders, but they did not know exactly what to anticipate. Paul Revere organized several spies and alarm riders to ride on horseback ahead of any

British troops who might advance to the west out of Boston. On the night of April 18, 1775, Revere and his spies waited in the dark streets of Boston for movement from the British. Meanwhile, General Gage had ordered Lieutenant Colonel Francis Smith to march 700 men to Concord to capture Hancock and Adams and to uncover stores of arms allegedly hidden there.

As Smith gathered his troops on Boston Common that evening, the patriots knew the soldiers would soon leave the city. But which way? Which road would they follow?

The British could either move north by boat and row across the water to Charlestown, or they could march south following the main road to Cambridge and then on to Lexington and Concord.

To get a closer look at troop movements, one of Revere's alarm riders, William Dawes, pretended he was a drunk farmer, staggering past British sentries. He saw what he needed to see. The British were planning to boat to Charlestown. This put them directly in a line headed straight to Paul Revere who was waiting impatiently in Charlestown.

Review and Write

How were the former members of the Massachusetts Assembly continuing to defy British law and authority even after their body was dissolved?

Midnight Riders

Paul Revere was one of Boston's most skilled silversmiths. His silver work was respected by many, yet sometimes he took other work, such as fashioning false teeth for willing clients. On the night of April 18, 1775, however, he was waiting in Charlestown just across the Charles River for a signal from his fellow patriots.

Earlier in the evening, Revere had left instructions to his comrades to signal his patriot friends in Charlestown of British intentions by lighting lanterns and placing them in the steeple of the city's Old North Church, which faced the river.

Revere said to look for either one lantern, which would indicate the British intended to march out of the southern end of the city, or the flicker of two lanterns which would signal to him that the British troops were headed in his direction. Once Dawes signaled the British route, he mounted his horse and rode out the southern end of Boston and on to Lexington, warning Minutemen and other militia along his route that the British were on the march.

Once the rebels placed two lanterns in the belfry of the church, Revere rowed across the Charles River in a small boat, a dangerous move, since British patrols were everywhere. (According to legend, Revere used the petticoats of a lady friend to wrap around his oars, intending to muffle their sound.) In Charlestown, Revere mounted his horse, spurred hard, and began his famous ride along a different road than that taken by Billy Dawes. Revere's shouts awoke his fellow patriots, who began to appear out of the darkness and headed for Lexington.

Revere had rowed out of Boston about 10 P.M. Two hours later, he arrived at Lexington and managed to warn Sam Adams and John Hancock. Two other alarm riders, William Dawes and Dr. Samuel Prescott met Revere at Lexington. (Prescott had spent the evening in Lexington, visiting a lady friend.) Now the three men rode on toward Concord. The time was now 1 A.M. While on their way, the three patriot riders were surprised and intercepted by a British cavalry patrol. In the darkness, both Dawes and Dr. Prescott managed to escape, but the British captured Revere. Of the three men, only Prescott managed to make it to Concord.

The British, uncertain of Revere's role and unclear what to do with him, allowed the Boston silversmith to go free, but they kept his horse. Revere then set out on foot and met with Adams and Hancock, the three of them finding their way to another small town, Burlington. (Revere later returned to Lexington to retrieve papers which Hancock had left behind in a trunk.)

While the rides of the three alarm riders— Revere, Dawes, and Prescott—had allowed the patriots to remove their hidden caches of arms and to warn Adams and Hancock, the British were still approaching. Hundreds of armed British regular troops were on their way and would soon encounter determined Massachusetts militiamen, ready to defend their leaders, their villages, and their cause.

Review and Write

How important were the efforts of Dawes, Prescott, and Revere on the night of April 18–19 on behalf of their fellow patriots?

The Battle of Lexington

Throughout the night of April 18-19, hundreds of British troops marched across the Massachusetts countryside toward the town of Concord. While the distance from Boston to Concord was only 20 miles, the march extended until daylight on the morning of April 19.

About dawn, a British Major, John Pitcairn, arrived with his weary soldiers at Lexington. There he was met by a group of Minutemen standing in double-line formation on the village green. Their immediate commander was a Captain John Parker.

These Lexington militiamen had answered the call of Paul Revere during the night as he rode into their little town. The men had remained awake through the entire night, waiting for the British troops to arrive. Before the arrival of the redcoats, Parker and his men had made a decision—they would not let the British pass into their town.

At daybreak, the waiting militiamen heard the sound of horse-hooves, as a scout, Thaddeus Bowman, approached them along a road which led from Cambridge. Bowman reported to Parker that the British were just a few miles away, numbering in the hundreds, nearly 1,000. Bowman estimated the arrival of the British troops at less than an hour.

As the morning began, the townspeople of Lexington appeared, some gathering in the local church; other in a drinking establishment, the Buckman Tavern. Still others took positions behind a granite and stone fence to the right of the Minutemen assembled on the village green.

In a short while, British troops began to appear on the road in front of the anxious rebels. One militiaman, John Robbins, later wrote: "There appeared a number of the King's troops, about a thousand as I thought, at the distance of about sixty or seventy yards from us, huzzaing (shouting), and on a quick pace towards us."

There was a tension in the air, but this kind of encounter between colonial militia and British regulars had taken place several times in previous months. With each previous encounter, shots had never been exchanged. With every previous confrontation, British troops had always yielded, choosing to avoid a fight. On this morning, Captain Parker expected the same circumstances to occur. Nevertheless, he instructed his men: "Stand your ground; don't fire unless fired upon, but if they mean to have a war, let it begin here."

As the Minutemen watched, however, the British did not appear ready to back down. In fact, they appeared to increase their marching step, heading straight for the waiting militiamen. Captain Parker made a quick decision and ordered his men to disperse, intending them to take cover behind a stone fence to their right.

Parker watched as nearly three dozen British troops ran toward his men, their muskets and bayonets pointed toward the scattering militiamen. A royal marine drew his sword and shouted to his redcoated comrades: "Damn them, we will have them!"

As many of Parker's men were headed toward the granite fence to take up positions, another cry from the British side split the tense air: "Lay down your arms, you damned rebels!"

Then, out from amidst the confused sounds of shouts, the clanging of equipment, the brush of running feet, a shot rang out over the din of hostility between the British regulars and the colonial militia.

Review and Write

1. How was the encounter between British troops and rebel militiamen different at Lexington than the usual, previous colonial encounters between these two sides?

2. During the night of April 18-19, 1775, Lexington militiamen had been awakened by the call of the patriot rider, Paul Revere. How had the militiamen occupied themselves between the call of Revere and the arrival of British troops at Lexington?

The Battle of Concord Bridge

Someone had fired a gun. To this day, no one knows who. Immediately, the British opened fire as they formed up ranks. Major Pitcairn shouted orders for his men to stop, but many of his troops had already shot the single ball in each of their muskets and were attacking the colonists with fixed bayonets.

When the British officers finally managed to bring their men under control, Colonel Smith ordered the force to continue their march to Concord, the true goal of their foray into the Massachusetts countryside. As they left the field, eight militiamen lay dead and another nine wounded. For all practical purposes, the American Revolutionary War had begun as a tragic accident.

Over in nearby Concord, militiamen were preparing to make contact with the British redcoats. None of the ammunition and foodstuffs stored there remained, for the colonists had managed to remove it all before the arrival of the British. Had Colonel Smith been able to capture the rebel supplies, it would have made for a fine prize: 20,000 pounds of musket balls and cartridges, 50 reams of cartridge paper, 318 barrels of flour, 17,000 pounds of salt fish, and 35,000 pounds of rice.

The previous night, at 2:30 A.M., Dr. Samuel Prescott had reached the community and informed the local rebel militia of the approaching British soldiers. After the skirmish on Lexington green, a patriot rider named Reuben Brown had arrived on horseback informing his comrades of the shots fired at Lexington. The local commander, Colonel James Barrett, began assembling his men for action.

By 8:30 A.M., British commander Smith arrived with his troops and began making a house-to-house search. When no weapons were found, he sent one company to guard the South Bridge and seven to guard the North Bridge over the Concord River. Another four companies were dispatched to Colonel Barrett's farm.

Barrett, in the meantime, kept his cool. He saw no reason to attack the British prematurely, knowing full well that additional militia and Minutemen

were on their way, numbering in the thousands. Only when Barrett and his men saw smoke rising above the town did the men act. (The British set fire to some cannon mounts they had discovered in the Concord courthouse.) Thinking the British were destroying their homes, an officer under Barrett asked his superior: "Will you let them burn the town down?" Barrett ordered his men to begin marching toward the town.

When Barrett's 400 men reached the North Bridge, they found 120 British soldiers guarding it. As the Americans advanced, the British did not intend to open fire. In fact, the troops on both sides were under orders not to fire first. But as the militia came closer and closer, the British commander, Captain Walter Laurie, retreated his men to the opposite side of the bridge. The Americans continued marching, in columns of two, toward the bridge. With few options, the British aimed their muskets, holding their fire until the first American troops put their boots on the bridge. The British fired warning shots, which failed to stop the approaching militia. Then, a volley of British bullets ripped into the menacing American line, dropping several men.

At last, an American officer, Major Buttrick, shouted: "Fire fellow soldiers, for God's sake, fire!" In the face of a withering musket barrage, the British abandoned Concord's North Bridge. The first day of fighting of the American Revolution was not over. Before the day ended, scores of soldiers on both sides would lie dead. And the killing would not stop for another six years.

Test VI

Part I.

Matching. *Match the answers shown below with the statements given above. Place the letters of the correct answers in the spaces below.*

1. British prime minister as of 1762 who believed the English colonies should be taxed
2. Parliamentary act of 1764 which increased duties on wines, coffee, sugar, and indigo
3. Parliamentary act of 1765 requiring an affixation on most printed materials in the colonies
4. Author of political tract titled *The Rights of the British Colonies Asserted and Proved*
5. Fiery Virginia speaker who proposed the Virginia Stamp Act Resolves in May, 1765
6. Stamp distributor who was intimidated by a mob that hanged him in effigy
7. Another name for a nonimportation agreement
8. British Chancellor of the Exchequer who promoted new taxes on the colonies in 1767
9. Royal governor who, in 1768, dissolved the Massachusetts assembly
10. Site of the Boston Massacre in March, 1770
11. British customs ship burned by local colonists after running aground in 1772
12. Royal governor of Massachusetts during the Boston Tea Party

A. *Gaspee* Incident	B. Francis Bernard	C. Andrew Oliver	D. Sugar Act
E. Stamp Act	F. boycott	G. Patrick Henry	H. Thomas Hutchinson
I. Customs House	J. Townshend	K. James Otis	L. George Grenville

1. ____ 2. ____ 3. ____ 4. ____ 5. ____ 6. ____ 7. ____ 8. ____ 9. ____ 10. ____ 11. ____ 12. ____

Part II.

Matching. *Match the answers shown below with the statements given above. Place the letters of the correct answers in the spaces below.*

1. Patriot leader who said the words: "Give me liberty, or give me death!"
2. Intercolonial body which held meetings in Philadelphia between 1774 and 1775
3. Boston silversmith who warned the Minutemen of the British approach in April 1775
4. One of two patriot leaders the British searched Concord for in April of 1775
5. Site of the warning lanterns in Boston on the night of April 18, 1775
6. British officer ordered to Concord to round up patriot leaders in April of 1775
7. This town was along the way as the British marched toward Concord in April of 1775
8. Militia commander of American troops on the Lexington Green on April 19, 1775
9. Site of armed clash in Concord between colonial militiamen and British regular troops
10. Patriot leader who campaigned against Sugar and Stamp Acts; was once Boston's junk dealer
11. Patriot leader who defended the British accused of murder after the Boston Massacre
12. Colonial group who typically remained loyal toward Great Britain

A. John Adams	B. John Parker	C. Old North Church	D. Paul Revere
E. Anglicans	F. North Bridge	G. Francis Smith	H. First Continental Congress
I. Samuel Adams	J. Lexington	K. John Hancock	L. Patrick Henry

1. ____ 2. ____ 3. ____ 4. ____ 5. ____ 6. ____ 7. ____ 8. ____ 9. ____ 10. ____ 11. ____ 12. ____

The Thirteen Colonies

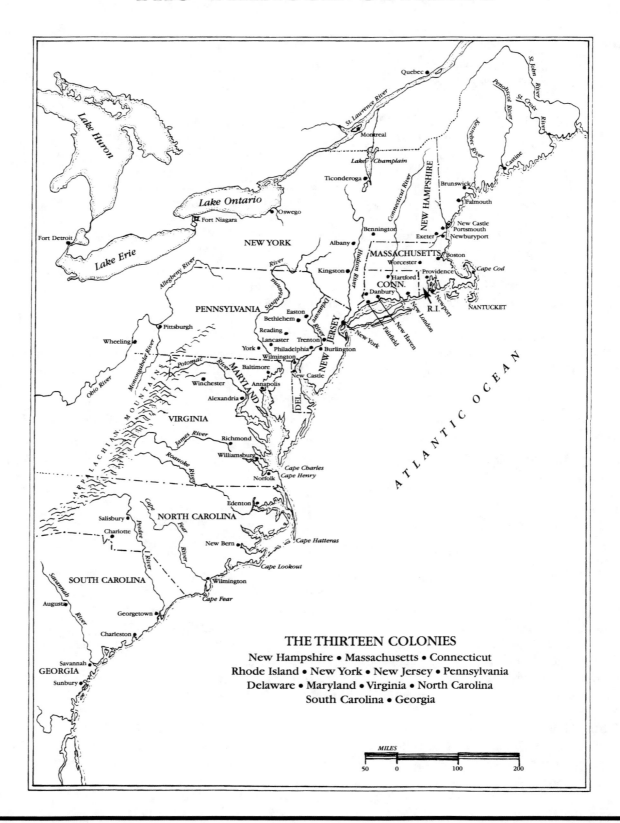

THE THIRTEEN COLONIES

New Hampshire • Massachusetts • Connecticut
Rhode Island • New York • New Jersey • Pennsylvania
Delaware • Maryland • Virginia • North Carolina
South Carolina • Georgia

The Colonial Economy 1750

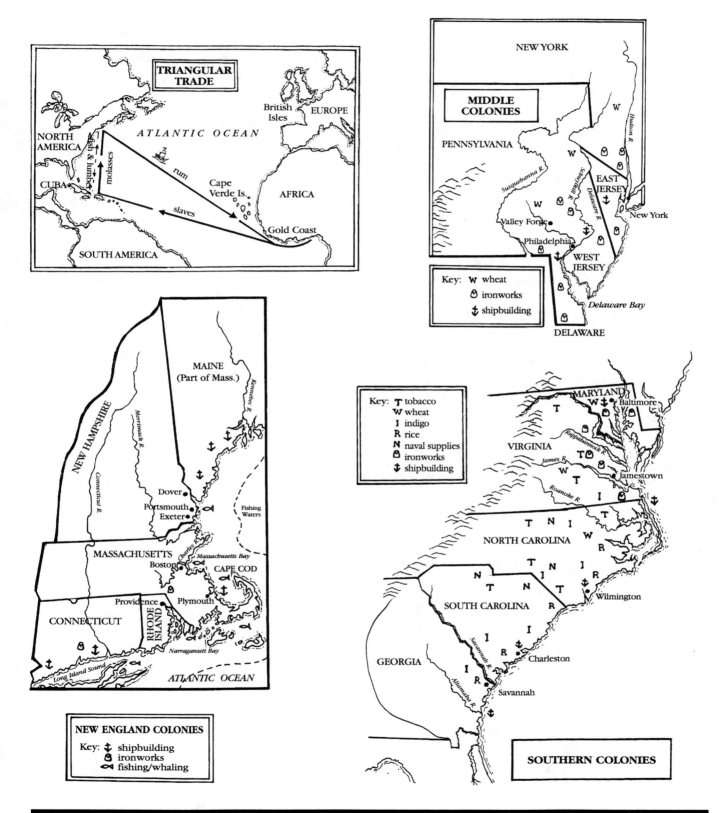

TRIANGULAR TRADE

ATLANTIC OCEAN

NORTH AMERICA

British Isles   EUROPE

CUBA   molasses   rum   Cape Verde Is.   AFRICA

slaves   Gold Coast

SOUTH AMERICA

fish & lumber

MIDDLE COLONIES

NEW YORK

PENNSYLVANIA

Susquehanna R.   Schuylkill R.   Hudson R.   Delaware R.

EAST JERSEY

Valley Forge

Philadelphia   WEST JERSEY

New York

Delaware Bay

DELAWARE

Key: W wheat
      ⚒ ironworks
      ⚓ shipbuilding

MAINE (Part of Mass.)

NEW HAMPSHIRE

Merrimack R.   Connecticut R.   Kennebec R.

Dover
Portsmouth
Exeter

Fishing Waters

MASSACHUSETTS

Charles R.   Massachusetts Bay

Boston   CAPE COD

Providence   Plymouth

CONNECTICUT   RHODE ISLAND

Narragansett Bay

Long Island Sound

ATLANTIC OCEAN

NEW ENGLAND COLONIES

Key: ⚓ shipbuilding
      ⚒ ironworks
      🐟 fishing/whaling

Key: T tobacco
      W wheat
      I indigo
      R rice
      N naval supplies
      ⚒ ironworks
      ⚓ shipbuilding

MARYLAND   Baltimore

VIRGINIA   Rappahannock R.

James R.   Jamestown

Roanoke R.

NORTH CAROLINA

SOUTH CAROLINA

Wilmington

Savannah R.

Charleston

GEORGIA

Altamaha R.   Savannah

SOUTHERN COLONIES

Answers

Page 2

1. Disputes between colonists, resulting in the murder of their leader; Indians stopped feeding the colonists; sickness; not enough tools with which to farm; many of those among the party did not intend to become farmers.

2. Ribaut met with local Indians and made peaceful relations with them. He traded with them regularly which provided food for the colonists at Charlesfort.

3. Ribaut sailed to France to get fresh provisions.

Page 3

1. Fort Caroline was established as a base for menacing Spanish treasure ships that sailed in nearby waters.

2. The losses of both Charlesfort and Fort Caroline brought an end to any serious French colonial efforts in the New World for the remainder of the 1500s.

Page 4

Hawkins sailed to the Spanish Caribbean in 1562 and sold black slaves he had picked up on an earlier voyage to West Africa to Spanish plantation owners. Also, Hawkins fought Spanish ships in pitched naval battles.

Page 5

Among their purposes for sailing to North America were a search for the Northwest Passage (there wasn't one) and to search for gold (there wasn't much to find). Also, attempts to establish colonies proved difficult.

Page 6

1. A proprietary colony would be operated by a proprietor, a leader who governed his lands in the name of the English king or queen, and profited from the colony.

2. Raleigh requested the right to take over his half-brother's charter to establish a colony in the New World.

Page 7

1. The colonists relied too heavily on food from the local Indians. When the natives became concerned about their dwindling supply, the food was cut off.

2. To make the new colony more appealing to would-be emigrants, Raleigh allowed not only men to participate but their wives, children, and their servants.

Page 8

Relations with local Native Americans deteriorated, causing the Indians to turn on the colonists. This was due to generally poor treatment of the Native Americans by the English colonists.

Page 9

Among those occupations listed which might have served the colony well would be common laborers, surgeon, blacksmith, sailors, carpenter, minister, bricklayers, soldiers, sea captain. The value of such skills as barber, perfumer, tailor, or goldsmith might be more difficult to argue. Students might include any one of these skills in either category, but each student should be ready to defend his or her choices.

Page 10

They arrived in the New World too late to plant an early crop; Since the colony was established in a low, swampy region, malaria-carrying mosquitoes infected the men; Bad water caused disease; The colonists consumed too much food on the voyage, making supplies scarce when they arrived; Many of the colonists were gentlemen, unaccustomed to work, so they expected others to do the labor; Many of the men were intent on searching for gold, so they did not work.

Page 11

1. After Smith left the colony, there was little true leadership or order within the settlement.

2. Just as the colonists were preparing to abandon the colony, a fleet of ships carrying supplies and new colonists arrived.

3. Of the first 300 colonists who came to Virginia and lived in Fort James, only 80 remained alive by the summer of 1609. Because of the dwindling numbers, the London Company waged a recruitment campaign which delivered 400 new colonists by August of 1609. Following a difficult winter of starvation and disease, Jamestown's population by the spring of 1610 was down to 60 colonists.

Page 12

1. Tobacco proved profitable and popular in the colony, giving colonists a source of income for their efforts in the New World. With the introduction of the House of Burgesses, Englishmen in Jamestown were able to pass laws and partially govern themselves.

2. New rules of conduct were enacted including the implementation of martial or military rule. This saved the colony. Then, the colony began to spread out of the Jamestown settlement itself, where the colonists built fortified villages and raised plenty of food, ending their food shortages.

3. Rolfe introduced a new variety of tobacco to Jamestown which provided a cash crop for the colony. He also discovered that air-drying helped preserve the flavor of the tobacco.

Page 13

1. The work of one farmer could produce a crop as profitable as the work of six men from an equal number of acres of wheat. Tobacco became so profitable that the colonists used it in lieu of money.

2. An indentured servant was typically a colonist too poor to pay his or her passage to America. Instead, a wealthier colonist paid for the voyage, leaving the new arrival with a debt. He or she then signed an indenture, obligating him or her to work for their master for a period typically between four and seven years.

Page 14

The Marylanders immediately turned to tobacco cultivation; they found land already cleared of trees by Indians, who had earlier moved from the region. The land was rich for farming.

Page 15

1. Answers will vary. Students will probably consider Onate's actions against the Acoma Pueblo to be cruel and harsh, which included the slaughter of 800 men, women, and children.

2. Such explorers had searched for fountains of youth and cities of gold. But the searches were fruitless.

3. By the 1580s, Franciscan missionaries reentered the region of modern-day New Mexico not in search of great riches, but lost souls.

Page 16: Test I

Part I

1. E   2. I   3. A   4. J   5. B   6. K   7. C   8. F   9. D   10. L   11. H   12. G

Part II

1. L   2. E   3. A   4. J   5. F   6. B   7. H   8. G   9. K   10. C   11. D.   12. I

Page 17

The French Canadian colonization efforts were able to establish friendlier relations with northern Native Americans and they were able to establish a viable fur trading system with the Indians which allowed the trading posts and settlements to prosper and grow.

Page 18

1. Through diplomacy, French leaders negotiated trade treaties with the many tribes of Native Americans. They dispatched trade agents and French traders to live with the Indians, to instruct them in French customs and practices. The fur trade became the center of economic vitality. The French government encouraged families to settle in Acadia. Inhabitants (farmers) and seigneurs (wealthier land-owners) established settlements, which might include a manor house, a Catholic church, and a public building. Inhabitants were able to produce crops despite a short growing season. This settlement helped trappers and traders who ventured along rivers and lakes in search of beaver pelts.

2. One key to the success of Champlain's efforts in helping to colonize Canada for the French was his

understanding of the native Americans. He believed the French would never succeed in North America without help from the Indians. Thus, he established good relations with them. Through diplomacy, he negotiated trade treaties, sent agents and traders to live with the Indians, instructing them to learn the native practices and languages.

3. This was one of the first times Canadian Indians had seen firearms. From then on, Indian warfare would include firearms. Also, because the French fought against the Mohawks, a Haudenosaunee tribe, those tribes would then ally themselves with the English.

Page 19
1. The coureurs de bois hunted and traded in the forest regions of Canada. The voyageurs traveled further west out onto the Canadian Plains.

2. The fur trade would not have been nearly as profitable as it was in the 17th and 18th centuries had beaver not become such a fashionable material to wear in Europe.

3. French trappers became familiar with more and more territory to the west of Quebec. They learned the locations of rivers, forests, and lakes, discovering the best routes to take them further into the interior. As they reached new territory, forts were often erected to provide trading centers.

Page 20
Based on their travels, the two explorers claimed the entire region of the Mississippi River Valley for France.

Page 21
1. They had valuable information about the lands they had explored and claimed for France. They told of Indian stories about the mighty Mississippi River and of the Gulf of Mexico.

2. He prepared a party to explore further the region originally traversed by Marquette and Joliet.

3. In searching for the mouth of the Mississippi, La Salle mistakenly identified Matagorda Bay as the river's mouth. When his party landed, they were besieged by Indians. La Salle was eventually killed, and the colonists abandoned the colony altogether.

Page 22
Prior to 1566, Holland was dominated by the Spanish. Once the Dutch successfully revolted against their Spanish oppressors, they were free to expand their trade and shipping around the world.

Page 23
Hudson's explorations provided information which England followed up on by establishing a fur trading company named after him, the Hudson's Bay Company. As for the Dutch, they returned to the region of New York, where Hudson had sailed and established a trading post on an island near today's Albany, which they called Fort Orange.

Page 24
1. Elementary school bulletin boards present them as a funny dressed man and woman, wearing black and white clothing, including shoes with big gold buckles. They tend to know about the first Thanksgiving.

2. The Puritans wanted to "purify" the Church of England, by making it less formal. Puritans who began to believe that the Church of England would never be "purified" began to separate themselves from it completely, calling themselves "Separatists."

3. King Henry VIII allowed for a separate Christian church from Catholicism—the Church of England. This Protestant movement developed its own religious ideas and religious institutions. The Puritans hoped to one day change the Church of England and make it less formal. They wished to purify the church.

4. The Puritans believed in the eventual "purification" or reform of the Church of England. The Separatists no loner believed the Church of England would be reformed so they decided to "separate" from the religious body altogether.

Page 25
1. One of the Jamestown colonists, John Smith, wrote a book which served as a part of the developing Puritan dream of migrating to the New World and building a community of people with similar beliefs. Two of the sect's leaders, Brewster and Bradford, read Smith's book with great enthusiasm.

2. He was hired to explore the region of New England, survey it and draw detailed maps. He was also to look for a suitable site for a new English colony.

3. John Smith's book would serve as a part of the developing Puritan dream of migrating to the New World and building a community of people with similar beliefs. Two of the Puritans leaders, William Brewster and William Bradford, read Smith's book with great enthusiasm.

4. They contracted with the Virginia company of Plymouth, promised to build a colony, live together on common lands, and send the profits from their labor and trade with local Indians back to the company's investors.

Page 26
The Mayflower Compact was one of the first examples of a document recognizing self-government in North America.

Page 27
1. The Native Americans provided translators, taught the Pilgrims how to live off the New England landscape, gave instructions on where to fish and how to plant Indian corn.

2. Squanto had been taken on an English fishing vessel to England in 1605. He lived there until 1614, then returned to his native land, only to be kidnapped by an English sea captain. In time he escaped and returned to England, only to be returned once more the New England in 1619.

Page 28
Winthrop knew the key to his colony's survival lay in the delivery of much needed supplies and food to Salem from England. When their settlement site proved inadequate to support a large community of settlers, Winthrop moved many of his people south to a site named Boston, which proved more suitable than their previous occupation.

Page 29

1. A centrally located fireplace provided the indoor heat source and the means for cooking meals. The saltbox design included roofs steeper on one side than the other as a preventive to heavy snow accumulation.

2. The New England Way was a lifestyle and pattern of settlement that might resemble that of life in England, but unique to America. First houses were identical to those of England. Family life was always important in the development of the New England settlements. Typically, people in New England lived longer, had more children, and were healthier than those living in other 17th century settlements.

3. The houses had small windows, an entry door centered along the front side of the dwelling, staircase at the front entrance, central fireplace, four rooms on the first floor, window openings minimal, and two bedrooms upstairs.

Page 30

1. When the Massachusetts Bay Colony was established, only those who were members of the Massachusetts Bay Colony had the right to govern the colony. In 1629, all stockholders of the Massachusetts Bay Company agreed to either migrate to America and participate directly in the colony or sell their shares of investment. This meant that the colonists who migrated there had control of how the colony was to be governed.

2. It became clear that independent-minded Puritans would not easily follow those who rested comfortably in England.

3. It became the tradition for each Puritan town and village to send two men to the General Court, called deputies.

Page 31

Both Williams and Hutchinson represented a challenge to established Puritan authority.

Page 32: Test II

Part I
1. I   2. E   3. J   4. A   5. F   6. K   7. B   8. G   9. H   10. C   11. L   12. D

Part II
1. E   2. F   3. I   4. A   5. B   6. J   7. C   8. K   9. D   10. G   11. L   12. H

Page 33

1. The pressure to conform to the religious standards of the leaders of the Massachusetts Bay Colony and by the arrival of more and more people led some people in New England to begin building new colonies.

2. The pattern typically began with the founding of a settlement. A colony required a charter from the English monarch. By the time such a land grant became official, colonists were already living in a new colony.

3. The colony of Rhode Island was first populated by those who left the Massachusetts Bay colony,

including Roger Williams. In 1643, Williams went to England to obtain a charter from King Charles I. When Puritans overthrew King Charles, Williams was able to get his charter.

Page 34

A group of families banded together to establish a new town and approached the General Court for permission. Before granting permission, the Court examined each member of the group to ensure they were all Puritans. The proposed site was examined to make sure it could support the group. Once the General Court was assured of these things, they granted the land to the settlers.

Page 35

When violence erupted, it was not always as simple as whites versus Indians. Some tribes early on had allied with English settlers to gain new strength against another traditional Indian enemy. The result was a pattern of alliances and loyalties leading to the deaths of Indians at the hands of other Indians.

Page 36

1. Bacon is a problematic figure. While his opposition to established English authority in Jamestown might serve as an inspiration to future American patriots, he was heavy-handed with the Native Americans and campaigned against tribes with savagery and without provocation.

2. The old headright system had not provided land to those who came to America as indentured servants, who had to work for the one who had paid their passage to the New World. When their indentures ended, they still did not own land, so they migrated inland and took up land illegally as squatters.

Page 38

1. The people in general in Salem believed in the reality and existence of witches and of the Devil's power. It was natural for the citizens of the town to take any claims about such things seriously, since they took the subject itself seriously on a daily basis.

2. Between 1630 and 1700, the number of New England cases involving people accused of witchcraft was around 100. Of that number, approximately 40 resulted in the death of the accused, usually by hanging.

Page 40

The Dutch had forced their European neighbors, the Swedes, from their trading posts along the Delaware River in 1655.

Page 42

1. Penn was raised a rich gentleman's son of social rank. The Quakers did not recognize any ranks among men. They pursued a simple Christianity of equality. Penn also had intended to serve in the royal diplomatic corps, but instead, he became a proprietor of a New World colony as a haven for his fellow Quakers.

2. Penn intended his colony to be as idealistic as possible. Penn laid out the plan of government, called the Frame of Government. There was to be a deputy governor and a council of assistants, elected by the colony's freeholders, who were landowners. The Assembly voted to pass the Great Law, granting religious freedom. Penn purchased land from the local Indians to make for better relations. He also regulated the trade between Indians and colonists, to ensure the Indians did not get cheated.

Page 43

1. Penn organized the primary city of the colony, Philadelphia; He planned the community; He ordered beautiful trees be planted in his city to give it an attractive appearance.

2. Penn established his city as a series of interconnected rectangles. The streets were laid out in a checker-board pattern. He included open, public squares and green spaces not intended for public grazing pastures, but as firebreaks. As the streets were laid out, he ordered the most handsome-looking trees be retained.

3. Merchants were immediately attracted to Pennsylvania and they soon dominated the city of Philadelphia. Between 1682 and 1689, over 50 merchants and traders established businesses in the young city. Thirty more were in business by 1700.

4. Penn ran into trouble when he reduced the number of council members from 72 to 18. He also proved to be an unpopular colonial administrator. He was a micro-manager, insisting he oversee the smallest details of the colony. In time, the colonial assembly took control of the colony.

Page 44

The land that became Delaware was part of two colonies for several years, which probably served as a disincentive for migration to Delaware. The colony exchanged hands several times, as well, which confused prospective colonists, who did not know who might be running the colony at a later date.

Page 46

1. The work required of slaves laboring on sugar plantations and in sugar mills was so strenuous, that most slaves died within four or five years after their arrival in the New World, which necessitated their constant replacement.

2. Italian merchants bought and sold people from Eastern Europe, the Slavic peoples, as slaves. The word "slave" is taken from the word "Slav."

3. They imported thousands of black slaves to provide cheap labor. The work required of slaves laboring on sugar plantations and in sugar mills was so strenuous, that most slaves died within four or five years after their arrival in the New World.

Page 47

1. Portuguese controlled the slave trade through its first century, and the Dutch challenged their markets and became the most prolific slave trading country of the 1600s. The English traders played a significant role in the slave trade during the 1500s.

2. After 1730, the involvement increased dramatically. From 1731 to 1740, over 40,000 slaves were shipped across the Atlantic. During the 1740s, the number rose to nearly 60,000. By the 1760s, the tally had risen to 70,000.

Page 48

New England traders brought distilled rum and barrels of salted cod to Africa to trade for slaves.

Page 49

Answers will vary, but they will probably include the following: Kidnapped against their will, chained, stripped, separated from families, crammed below decks on slave ships in filthy conditions, with no sanitation.

Page 50: Test III

Part I:
1. E   2. I   3. A   4. F   5. B   6. J   7. C   8. K   9. G   10. L   11. D   12. H

Part II:
1. I   2. E   3. B   4. J   5. A   6. F   7. C   8. K   9. D   10. G   11. H   12. L

Page 51

1. The earliest African arrivals were not, by definition, true slaves, since the institution did not legally exist in North America. Thus, the early arrivals worked as indentured servants. Only later did slavery come into existence by Virginia law.

2. The availability of indentured servants began to decrease in the late 1600s and into the 1700s. Better economic times in England brought fewer young people anxious to come to America who did not have the money to pay their own way. Also, indentured servants were living longer, surviving their indentures. During the late 1600s, social conflicts, such as Bacon's Rebellion in the 1670s, which was led by former indentured servants in Virginia, led some planters to turn increasingly to black workers over a dwindling number of available indentured servants.

Page 54

1. Florida, the American Southwest from Texas to California, including modern-day Arizona and New Mexico.

2. The extreme control of the region by Mexico City officials. Trade laws restricted Spanish colonists to bartering their wool, buffalo hides, deerskins, and pottery for manufactured goods shipped from the capital of Viceroy.

3. By the 1680s, southern plains tribes had gained access to the horse through the Spanish. The introduction of the horse changed Plains life by allowing the tribes of that region to develop the horse and buffalo culture.

Page 55

1. While the English colonies were connected one to another, all hugging the Atlantic Coast, the French had established settlements spread out from Canada in the north to the Gulf of Mexico in the south.

2. By mid-1700s, the population of the British Atlantic colonies numbered nearly 1.2 million inhabitants. As late as 1750, the population of New France had increased to only 70,000.

Page 56

The Puritans would eventually give serious consideration to the idea of religious toleration. This change developed from within the Puritan faith, as Puritans challenged the tenets of Puritan beliefs.

Page 57

New England economy consisted of furs, fish, lumber, as well as merchandising, banking, shipbuilding, and shipping, as well as dried fish, livestock, wood products, whale-related products such as oil and spermaceti and cereal grains. In time, such products as furniture, clothing, and tableware were being produced in the New England colonies.

Page 58

1. Traffic jams and accidents

2. The economies of the Middle Colonies were dominated by the trade, shipping, and merchandising found in Philadelphia and New York City.

3. Flatbush was home to the Dutch; Huguenots (French Protestants) lived in New Rochelle; Bergen County continued the Flemish; while the Scots settled in Perth Amboy.

Page 59

1. Lack of available farmland; few roads connecting the colonies; precarious lives; Indian attack potential.

2. There was a need for those who migrated to America to remain within the vicinity of ocean-going ships, so they could receive regular deliveries of supplies and remain connected to Europe.

3. The Fall Line is a line running from New York City to Atlanta, Georgia, today. The line is a natural one, marked by rapids and waterfalls. It also serves as the furthest point inland that an ocean-going vessel of the period could travel upstream. It hindered western movement.

Page 60

Since plantations were common, people lived scattered out from one another. Cities were few and the standard pattern of settlement had resulted in the inhabitants dispersing along the river valleys, establishing their farms and plantations.

Page 62

1. When English colonists arrived in North America, they came with little support from English monarchs or Parliament.

2. Mercantilism occurs when the state directs all economic activities within its national and colonial borders with the intention of the state profiting first, followed by personal, private profit. It relies on a favorable balance of trade.

3. North America was full of natural resources such as lumber, furs, and iron which required a minimum of labor. England had plenty of workers who could produce labor-intensive products such as clothing, fancy furniture, and wrought iron.

Page 63: Test IV

Part I.
1. I   2. B   3. E   4. J   5. C   6. F   7. A   8. K   9. G   10. D   11. H   12. L

Part II.
1. L   2. D   3. H   4. A   5. I   6. G   7. B   8. J   9. C   10. E   11. F   12. K

Page 66
1. They began in Europe first than spread to the colonies.

2. French Canadians and their Indian allies raided New England and New York settlements, resulting in the deaths of hundreds of British colonists. Massachusetts troops captured the French fort of Louisburg on Cape Breton Island with the help of the British Navy.

Page 67
1. This interior region of North America lay west of the Appalachians, south of the Great Lakes to the Ohio River. Many rivers flowed into the Ohio, including the Monongahela, Allegheny, Tennessee, Cumberland, and Wabash.

2. The organization of English land speculation companies.

Page 68
Answers will vary. Washington appears to make serious mistakes in dealing with enemies. He is not able to restrain his Indian allies who kill French captives; he places Fort Necessity in a low place, allowing it to be flooded while the French and Indians are attacking.

Page 69
The delegates at the meeting were not yet ready to cooperate as colonies and surrender any independence to the wider authority.

Page 70
1. He moved slowly, having his men hack a trail through the woods. This eliminated the possibility of surprising the French. He also marched his men in wide columns. At one point, he sent his men along a narrow trail, allowing them to scatter along a thin line.

2. Washington helped facilitate the retreat of the British and his militia from the engagement. Braddock was killed and his body buried in the wilderness.

Page 71
Montcalm assembled more than 2500 French regular infantry, plus an equal number of Canadian militia, more than 1000 Indians and hundreds of additional military personnel. The French dug zigzag trenches and moved their canon and mortars close enough to blow the fort apart. After six days of shelling, the fort fell.

Page 73
1. While the British controlled both ends of the Saint Lawrence, they could not travel the length of the river, because Quebec dominated the river.

2. Very similar. Both armies marched toward the other in well-ordered columns, with the men firing in volleys.

Page 74
France ceded Canada to the British, effectively ending their colonial power in North America. France lost Louisiana to the Spanish, at Britain's insistence.

Page 75:

The British ministry attempted to alleviate some of the problems between the Indians and its colonies. In the fall of 1763, the British Crown declared the lands west of the Appalachian Mountains to be off limits to colonial migration and settlement.

Page 76: Test V

Part I.
1. L   2. B   3. E   4. C   5. I   6. F   7. J   8. A   9. G   10. D   11. K   12. H

Part II.
1. D   2. I   3. H   4. G   5. C   6. K   7. F   8. B   9. J   10. A   11. L   12. E

Page 77

1. The concept of actual representation demanded that voters physically vote for their representatives. Virtual representation allows for a body to represent a people even if they never voted for that body to exist.

2. Grenville doubled the number of British regular troops in the American colonies to 7500 men.

Page 79

James Otis claimed that Parliament could not tax the colonies, since Americans were not members of the English legislative. Otis suggested the question of Parliamentary authority was to give membership in Parliament to elected Americans. Henry directly opposed the Stamp Act.

Page 80

1. Answers will vary. Students will have to assess whether or not they would have supported the causes of the patriots and whether or not they might have protested in ways which constitute civil disobedience.

2. The Loyal Nine were a group of Boston printers, artisans, and distillers who organized a demonstration against the Stamp Act. They burned in effigy, the designated stamp distributor for Boston.

3. The Sons of Liberty rioted outside the homes of several customs officials. They attacked the townhouse of Thomas Hutchinson, then looted and destroyed his home. Ironically, Hutchinson did not even support the Stamp Act.

4. The colonies of New York, Massachusetts, Rhode Island, Connecticut, New Jersey, Maryland, and South Carolina attended the New York City conference and produced a unified written protest. The meeting was important because it represented the first attempt at intercolonial unification since the Albany Plan of Union.

Page 81

1. Colonists wrote pamphlets against both. Colonial legislatures protested and issued paper protests. Public demonstrations were waged against both. Boycotts were organized against both.

2. The Declaratory Act was passed. This act reminded everyone that Parliament had the ability to tax and legislate on behalf of Great Britain's colonies in America.

3. The Townshend Duties were a tax on imports to the colonies, such as paper, lead, glass, and tea. They were unpopular because, from the onset, these duties were designed to do nothing but raise money, not regulate trade.

Page 83
Adams wrote against British actions, helped organize demonstrations, called meetings, etc.

Page 84
1. Answers will vary. Colonists interpreted the measure as a cagey way of convincing the Americans to accept Parliamentary authority, since the cheaper tea would still be taxed under the last of the remaining Townshend duty laws.

2. The tax was so insignificant an amount that a colonist would have to drink a gallon of tea a day for a year before his tea tax bill would equal one dollar.

3. Under the customs law, the duty on the tea was to be paid within twenty days of a ship's docking or its cargo would be seized by customs officials.

4. Colonists disguised as Indians approached the tea ships, boarded them and threw the tea overboard. Lord North responded by ordering the closing of the harbor at Boston.

Page 85
1. Answers will vary.

2. 1) What were the colonies upset about? 2) What do they intend to do about it? 3) Is it time for a new relationship between England and the colonies?

Page 86
By the early 1770s, colonists no longer thought of themselves as English. They had forged a new identity—a spirit of independence, of social openness, of having the ability to work one's way up from nothing—these qualities had driven several generations to develop an "American" view of their world.

Page 87
They either wrote or spoke with a fiery spirit which constantly rallied support for the patriot causes.

Page 88
1. Answers will vary.

2. Adams estimated that approximately one-third of the colonists were in favor of the patriot cause, another third were loyal to Great Britain, and a final third were neutral.
3. Neutral groups: Quakers, many Scot-Irish

Page 89
1. The British are determined to stop patriot efforts possibly with a show of military force. Parliament and the Crown authorized monies to provide the dispatch of additional British troops to the colonies. The patriots are storing gunpowder and weapons, and militiamen and others are promising to support the patriot cause by signing pledges.

2. They had become convinced that the rebellion must be stopped, possibly with a show of military force.

3. They authorized monies to provide the dispatch of additional British regular troops to the colonies. High-ranking British generals were sent to the colonies to command British forces. Massachusetts was declared to be in a state of rebellion, giving British soldiers the right to fire upon any suspected patriot rebel, on sight.

Page 90

The House members had voted to collect colonial taxes for itself, and saw themselves as the true government of their colony. They also gave support to rebel militiamen.

Page 91

They provided the warnings for the rebels, allowing them to rally against the British, move supplies which might be captured by the British, and gave Sam Adams and John Hancock warning to escape.

Page 92

1. With each previous encounter, shots had never been exchanged. With every such previous confrontation, British troops had always yielded, choosing to avoid a fight.

2. The men had remained awake the entire night, waiting for the British troops to arrive. Before the arrival of the redcoats, the patriot commander and his men agreed to not allow the British to pass into their town.

Page 94: Test VI

Part I.
  1. L   2. D   3. E   4. K   5. G   6. C   7. F   8. J   9. B   10. I   11. A   12. H

Part II.
  1. L   2. H   3. D   4. K   5. C   6. G   7. J   8. B   9. F   10. I   11. A   12. E

Bibliography

Boorstin, Daniel. *The Americans: The National Experience* (New York: Random House, 1965).

Burney, Eugenia. *Colonial North Carolina* (Nashville: Thomas Nelson, Inc., 1975).

Cronin, William. *Changes in the Land: Indians, Colonists, and the Ecology of New England* (New York: Hill and Wang, 1983).

Dunn, Richard S. and Mary Maples Dunn, Eds. *The World of William Penn* {Philadelphia: University of Pennsylvania Press, 1986).

Earle, Alice Morse. *Home Life in Colonial Days* (Lee, Massachusetts: Berkshire House, 1993).

Edwards, C. P. Roger *Williams: Defender of Freedom* (Nashville: Abingdon Press, 1957).

Emerson, Caroline D. *Pioneer Children of America* (Boston: D. C. Heath and Company, 1965).

Flexner, James Thomas. *Washington: The Indispensable Man* (Boston: Little, Brown and Company, 1974).

Fradin, Dennis Brindell. *Anne Hutchinson: Fighter for Religious Freedom* (Berkeley Heights, NJ: Enslow Publishers, Inc., 1990).

—*The 13 Colonies Series* (Danbury, CT: Children's Press, 1986-1989).

Graff, Henry F. *The Free and the Brave* (Chicago: Rand McNally, 1977).

Hakim, Joy. *The First Americans* (New York: Oxford University Press, 1993).

—*From Colonies to Country* (New York: Oxford University Press, 1998).

—*Making Thirteen Colonies* (New York: Oxford University Press, 1998).

Hamilton, Edward P. *The French and Indian Wars* (Garden City, NY: Doubleday, 1962).

Harrison, Bird. *Battle for a Continent: The French and Indian War, 1754-1763* (New York: Oxford University Press, 1965).

Hawke, David. *The Colonial Experience* (Indianapolis: The Bobbs-Merrill Company, Inc., 1966).

Hoffer, Peter Charles. *The Brave New World: A History of Early America* (Boston: Houghton Mifflin, 2000).

Howarth, Sarah. *Colonial People* (Brookfield, CT: The Millbrook Press, 1994).

Hults, Dorothy N. *New Amsterdam Days and Ways* (New York: Harcourt Brace, 1963).

Josephy, Alvin M., Jr. *The Patriot Chiefs* (New York: Penguin Books, 1976).

Lacy, Dan. *The Colony of Virginia* (Danbury, CT: Franklin Watts Ltd., 1973).

Malone, Dumas. Ed. *"William Penn." Dictionary of American Biography* (New York: Charles Scribner"s Sons, 1934. 433-437).

McGovern, Ann. *If You Lived in Colonial Times* (New York: Scholastic, Inc., 1992).

McNeese, Tim. *From Trails to Turnpikes* (New York: Crestwood House, 1993).

Meltzer, Milton. *Milestones to American Liberty: The Foundations of the Republic* (New York: Thomas Y. Crowell Company, 1965).

Milner, Clyde A. II. *The Oxford History of the American West* (New York: Oxford University Press, 1994).

Minks, Benton and Louise. *The French and Indian War* (San Diego: Lucent Books, 1995).

Morison, Samuel Eliot. *Builders of the Bay Colony* (Boston: Houghton Mifflin, 1930).

—*The European Discovery of America: The Southern Voyages, A.D. 1492-1616* (New York: Oxford University Press, 1974).

—*The Oxford History of the American People* (New York: Oxford University Press, 1965).

Nash, Gary B. *Red, White and Black: The Peoples of Early America* (Englewood Cliffs, NJ: Prentice-Hall, 1982).

Parkman, Francis. Montcalm and Wolfe. *[France and England in North America, Part Seventh], Vol. III.* (Boston: Little, Brown, 1902).

Rich, L.D. *King Phillip"s War, 1675-76* (Danbury, CT: Franklin Watts Ltd., 1972).

Russell, Francis. *The French and Indian Wars* (New York: American Heritage, 1962).

Smith, Carter. *Sourcebooks on Colonial America* (Brookfield, CT: The Millbrook Press, 1991).

Tunis, Edwin. *Colonial Craftsmen and the Beginnings of American Industry* (Cleveland: The World Publishing Company, 1965).

—*Colonial Living* (Cleveland: The World Publishing Company, 1957).

—*Frontier Living* (New York: Thomas Crowell, 1961).

Warner, John F. *Colonial American Home Life* (Danbury, CT: Franklin Watts Ltd., 1993).

Weinstein, Allen and R. Jackson Wilson. *Freedom and Crisis: An American History* (New York: Random House, 1974).

Williams, Selma R. *Kings, Commoners, & Colonists* (New York: Atheneum, 1974).

Woodhead, Henry, Ed. *Realm of the Iroquois* (Alexandria, VA: Time-Life Books, 1993).